The Benefits of Being A Vegetarian

The Benefits of Being A Vegetarian

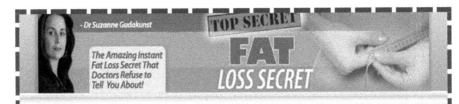

World-Famous TV Lady Doctor comes forth and blows the lid off the conspiracy to keep you unhealthy, fat & just plain sick...

Shocking Proof!

Here's the real reason you're fat...

"The Reason You Can't Lose Weight has Nothing to Do With Your *Will-Power, Over-Eating* or the *Right Diet!* ... The Reason You are Fat and Unhealthy is Because You Have Disgusting *Plaque* and Horrible Little *'CRITTERS'* Living in Your Guts!"

"...And Now I'm Going to Show You How to Get Rid of All of It so You Can Shed 10 lbs, 25 lbs, 50 lbs even 100 lbs or more - and Keep It Off FOREVER!!"

TOP SECRET
Fat Loss Secret

DOWNLOAD NOW

The Benefits of Being A Vegetarian

Contents

Eliminate poultry:

What Does A Vegan Use Instead Of Gelatin

So many dishes are made with gelatin. They include many summer favorites. Both sweet and savory dishes have been based on gelatin.

Children love fruit flavored gelatin based dishes such as jello. A more adult dinner table can be graced with a salad in a gelatin mould. Mousses and cheesecakes can both call for gelatin.

So what can a vegan or a strict vegetarian use who wants to avoid animal products. Even meat eaters may wish to use an alternative to gelatin for health reasons.

Gelatin is derived from beef or pork. Cooks sometimes make their own by boiling bones or pigs' trotters but most often it is bought in powder form ready made in packets. It can then simply be added to water that is just below boiling point. This provides the basis for a whole range of jellied dishes.

A vegan or vegetarian can use rice starch, arrowroot or potato starch for some of these dishes. A fruit or vegetable flan can be covered in a jelly like glaze by blending a little of one of these products with water and then adding it to boiling water. It is important to stir the mixture vigorously to prevent lumps forming. If lumps do form use a food processor to remove them.

But for a molded jelly shape you will need something different. A seaweed based product called agar-agar is the thing to use here. This can be bought in powder form and added to hot water just like gelatin. It is even available to buy it in flavored forms that will make the traditional jello that children and many adults love.

Be careful not to keep an agar-agar jelly too long. They should be eaten on the same day as they are made because they provide an ideal environment for bacteria to grow

But they are quick to make and quicker than gelatin to set. So it is not really a problem to make one quickly just before you need it.

In powder form agar- agar will keep for months. That makes it a good stand by to keep in your store cupboard.

Many non-vegetarians will find it useful to keep some handy for visiting vegetarians. In many ways it is easier to use than gelatin which can easily go "stringy" if the water used is too hot. Agar-agar is almost fool proof.

Vegetarianism And Cancer: The Evidence

Vegetarianism has the reputation of being a healthy diet because it is low in fat and high in vegetable products and fibre. An increasing number of scientific studies are showing that a vegetarian diet can help to prevent cancer and can assist the body to recover from cancer when combined with chemo-therapy or radiation therapy.

A vegetarian diet is not an alternative to conventional forms of treatment. It would be unwise to reject medical treatments that have been shown to work. Only the irresponsible would recommend a cancer patient to reject conventional medical treatment.

What a vegetarian diet can do for a patient who is undergoing cancer treatment is to help their body cope with the side effects. A diet high in natural fruit and vegetable juices will provide the body with important nutrients that help the natural healing process.

Patients who adopt a vegetarian diet often report an improvement in their general outlook and their attitude to the disease. In part this may be because they are eating a nutrient rich diet.

But the psychological effect of switching to a vegetarian diet can be as important as the nutritional value. Cancer patients suffer from a feeling of loss of control because their whole life becomes dominated by a complex regime of treatment that is in the hands of specialists. When they change to a vegetarian diet they regain their sense of control over their own lives.

The effect of psychology on disease should never be underestimated. It is well documented in the medical literature as the placebo effect. Feeling better should not be dismissed in cancer treatment. Vegetarianism will do not harm and it may do some good.

But it is in cancer prevention that the benefits of vegetarianism are most thoroughly documented. A diet which contains many soya based products has been shown to be associated with a low risk of cancer. Breast cancer in particular is very rare among women who eat a soy based diet. Vegetarianism is the soy based diet par excellence.

Diets which are high in meat, especially red meat like beef, has been shown to be associated with a higher incidence of colon cancer. Animal fat may also be associated with a higher level of breast cancer in younger women. Dairy products may be associated with an elevated risk of ovarian cancer.

A vegetarian diet alone can never eliminate the risk of cancer because there are so many environmental and genetic factors involved. But it can reduce the risk because it is high in fruit and vegetables that contain substances called flavonoids and other antioxidants that destroy the free radicals which can cause cancer.

Free radicals are molecules that damage the DNA of cells. We are exposed to free radicals through pollution as well as diet so they are almost impossible to avoid. But by eating a vegetarian diet that is rich in fruit in vegetables we can help our bodies to resist their effects.

Vegetarians and Non-Vegetarians can Enjoy Tofu

Tofu is often a object of fun. Those who have never eaten it often laugh at it. Even some vegetarians hesitate to try it because they fear that they may be ridiculed or simply do not know how to cook it.

But tofu is a highly nutritious food that can be cooked in variety of delicious ways. Vegetarians and non-vegetarians can enjoy it. What is more it has proven health benefits.

Tofu comes in two forms. There is silken tofu which you will find on the supermarket shelf with oriental foods. Silken tofu can be kept for a long time without refrigeration if the packet is unopened. Once opened it must be stored in the fridge.

You will find regular tofu in the chiller department of you supermarket. It usually comes in a plastic vacuum pack.

Both kinds of tofu come in a white block. It looks something like cheese. Silken tofu is widely used in Japanese cooking but both kinds of tofu can be used in most dishes that call for tofu.

When you taste tofu you will discover that there is no comparison with cheese. it tastes of nothing. That is the secret of cooking tofu. You are adding the flavor. The advantage is that tofu is endlessly adaptable. It takes on the flavor of the herbs, spices and vegetables with which it is cook ed.

You can use it in stir fries by cutting it into little cubes. Flavor it with garlic, ginger, sesame oil, chilies or whatever you like to add to your favorite stir fry. If you keep a block of silken tofu in the store cupboard you will always have something make a stir fry in a hurry.

Tofu can also be used for salad dressings and creamy sauces for savory or sweet dishes. Throw either kind in the food processor with the flavorings you want to use. For a salad dressing choose garlic, lemon juice, honey or herbs. if you make the same dressing thicker it can be used as a spread or dip.

You might like to try it as a filling in baked potato. Roasted vegetables with a tofu dip make a delicious first course or snack meal.

A thick paste of tofu can even be made into a burger and served in a bun. It is an ideal vegetarian option for the barbecue.

For a sweet sauce add some honey, cinnamon perhaps, nutmeg, even chocolate or pureed fruit. You can use the same mixture for a cheesecake recipe if you make it a little stiffer than you would for a sauce. A few chopped nuts sprinkled on top add a variety of texture.

Tofu is a very healthy food. It is low in fat and contains no animal fat at all. It will not raise your cholesterol levels and is reputed to play a part in raising the level of "good" cholesterol.

The isoflavones found in soya based products such as tofu are thought to play a part in reducing the risk of cancer because they combat free radicals in the body.

Whether you use tofu as part of a vegetarian diet or a non-vegetarian diet it is a food worthy trying.

Why Should You Become A Vegetarian?

There are three basic reasons why you should become a vegetarian. Firstly, a vegetarian diet is good for your health. Secondly, it is a contribution to the welfare of animals. Thirdly, becoming a vegetarian is good for the environment.

Let's start with your health. By eating a vegetarian diet you will consume considerably less saturated fat than by eating a conventional meat based diet. This will be good for the health of your heart.

Studies have shown that people who eat nuts on a regular basis are less likely to suffer heart attacks. Vegetarians depend on nuts as one of their sources of protein. Heart disease has become a major killer in all modern industrialized societies.

That alone would be a major reason to consider becoming a vegetarian. But the health benefits are even greater than that. Vegetarians are seldom obese. Obesity and the health problems associated with it have become a major public health issue.

Most vegetarians consume a lot of complex carbohydrates. These are the "good carbs" you will have heard of that do not cause rapid fluctuations in blood sugar levels. When we experience a rush of blood sugar we must produce more insulin. If this process is repeated our bodies can become insensitive to our own insulin and type 2 diabetes may result in extreme cases. Type 2 diabetes is becoming increasingly common even in comparatively young people because of the modern diet.

Cancer is another killer disease that is on the increase. A vegetarian diet can play a part in reducing the risk of some cancers because it is high in fibre and high anti-oxidants that combat free radicals.

By eliminating meat from your diet as a vegetarian you are reducing your exposure to antibiotics that are used in animal husbandry and to the hormones that are used as growth promoters and to increase milk production. Antibiotics in food can result in antibiotic resistance. Hormones fed to animals can disrupt the activity of the hormones that our own bodies produce.

The intensive production of animals in factory farming systems raises major issues of animal welfare. There are also environmental concerns because factory farming is so resource hungry. Vast amounts of land are used to produce animal feed that could be used more efficiently to produce food for people. If more of us were vegetarians fewer children would go to bed hungry.

By becoming a vegetarian you are contributing to your own health, to the welfare of other people, to the welfare of animals and to the health of the planet. As an individual your contribution may be small, but your decision to become a vegetarian will influence others.

Can You Really Switch To Vegetarianism During Your Pregnancy?

Pregnancy brings a new responsibility. You have charge of the health and well being of another human being. For many of us it is the time when we give up high risk activities like drinking and smoking. A major change in diet sounds risky too, but changing to a vegetarian diet in pregnancy really should not be seen in that light. Taken slowly and sensibly changing to vegetarianism during pregnancy is quite safe.

You should, of course, discuss your diet and any changes you plan to make to it with your health care professional. If they see that you are taking the process seriously they will probably be supportive of your decision to change to vegetarianism during pregnancy.

If you approach becoming a vegetarian seriously it will benefit both you and your baby. A typical vegetarian eats far less junk food than most people. They are more likely to prepare meals from basic ingredients and to consume a wide variety of vegetables, fruit, nuts, pulses and grains than people who eat processed food. If you are not totally vegan then you will also be eating dairy produce such as milk and cheese and eggs. That should ensure you a balanced diet.

In pregnancy a woman has special dietary needs. A pregnant woman only needs about 300 extra calories a day and between 10 and 16 grams of extra protein. But it is important to ensure that you get enough folic acid, iron, zinc and vitamin B-12. Leafy green vegetables are useful here. As a vegetarian you will probably get more of these than on a typical modern diet. Your health professional will be on the look out for deficiencies. It will help them to know that you are vegetarian. Discuss whether you need dietary supplements.

Going vegetarian presents your body with many challenges. So it is important to take it slowly. This is true at any time, but it is especially true when you plan to go vegetarian during pregnancy. The best advice is to take it slowly. Make the transition gradually by eating vegetarian one or two days a week at first. This allows your body to detoxify itself slowly.

Taking things step by step also allows you to introduce new sources of protein into your diet gradually. It will give you chance to learn how to use plant based proteins like soya. There's an art to making a good tofu burger or a tasty lentil soup. Changing your shopping habits takes time too.

Something else to consider when changing to a vegetarian diet during pregnancy is the need for exercise and sunlight. Sunlight is necessary for your body to manufacture its own vitamin D. A dietary supplement may be necessary depending where you live and the time of year.

At any time the transition to vegetarianism should be about achieving a healthy life style. This is especially true when the change to vegetarianism is made during pregnancy. Going vegetarian during pregnancy is perfectly possible provided that you do so carefully and in consultation with your health professional. Above all listen to your own body. The transition to vegetarianism during your pregnancy can be beneficial to both you and your baby.

When Milk Is Not A Healthy Food

Milk is often praised as a perfect food which contains all the protein, fats and minerals that are needed for a healthy life. It is often recommended that we drink a pint of milk a day.

Milk is, after all, the only food for the young of mammals. It seems natural that we should rely on it and other dairy produce manufactured from milk as a source of nutrition.

But matters are not so straightforward. Cows' milk is not a natural food for human beings. For human infants it can be harmful unless modified as it is infant formula.

Older children can often tolerate milk, but many adults lose the stomach enzyme that allows them to digest milk. In northern latitudes many adults retain that enzyme and they can digest milk. But in other parts of the world adults seldom have the ability to do so.
As societies become more diverse it is not uncommon to encounter individuals who cannot tolerate milk in their diet.

Even those of us who can drink milk need to be aware of health concerns that are linked to a high consumption of milk and dairy produce. Full cream milk can help to raise the body's level of cholesterol because it contains animal fat. This is even more true of cheese, butter and cream, which contain a higher proportion of fat.

Skimmed milk may be answer to this problem but a high consumption of dairy foods has been associated with various forms of cancer. Breast cancer, ovarian cancer and prostate cancer have all been linked to dairy foods. A Harvard study showed that if too much dairy produce is consumed the body's enzymes may not be able to break down the lactose that milk contains. This can build up in the blood stream and contribute to cancer formation in the body's organs.

Milk produced under modern factory farming conditions is a long way from the milk that used to be available. Cows do not necessarily graze on grass. They may be kept indoors and fed on concentrates. This has several consequences for their milk. Milk from grass fed cattle is typically high in vitamin D. But milk from cattle reared indoors is not.

Vitamin D is essential if we are to utilize calcium in bone growth and repair. We may be drinking milk in the belief that it helps us avoid osteoporosis when in fact it does not. Milk is not a reliable source of either vitamin D or calcium.

Milk can also contain high levels of hormones such as IGF-I. This substance has been linked to a number of cancers.

It is possible to avoid milk and still obtain sufficient nutrients from a variety of other sources. Leafy green vegetables and whole grains are a good source of calcium. Vegetables such as carrots are a good source of vitamin D. Soya products contain no animal fat and are often fortified with both vitamin D and calcium.

The Importance Of Eating A Healthful Vegetarian Diet

So often when people say they are vegetarian they mean that they do not eat meat. But being a vegetarian is about more than just not eating meat. It is possible to be a vegetarian in the sense of not eating meat and eat a very unhealthy diet indeed.

A vegetarian diet may by high in cholesterol if it relies too much on cheese and eggs. It may be low in fibre if it is based on refined grain products like white bread, white pasta and white rice. If it lacks fresh vegetables you diet will be deficient in vitamins and minerals. You may vegetarian but you may not be eating a healthful vegetarian diet.

Going vegetarian is about more than just not eating meat. It means taking a positive decision to eat a wide range of foods that provide a balanced mixture of nutrients.

It is important to plan the change to a vegetarian diet. This may mean buying some new equipment for your kitchen. If you are used to eating convenience foods you may need to buy some basic items.

The next step is to plan your meals. Not all vegetarian meals rely on cheese, eggs and milk for protein. These are useful ingredients in a vegetarian diet but not by any means essential. It is perfectly possible to get enough protein by combining grains with pulse such as peas, beans and lentils. A bowl of lentil soup with a slice of bread provides all the essential amino you need. Chili beans and rice combine in the same way to create what is called a complete protein.

A diet based on pulses and whole grains has the immense of advantage of providing you with enough fibre. This is important to maintain colon health. Cancer of the colon is most common among people who eat a diet based on over-refined processed foods. Fibre is one of the key ingredients in a healthful vegetarian diet.

Switching to a high fibre diet takes a little time. Your body needs to adjust. So take things slowly at first.

A healthful vegetarian diet based on whole grains, pulses, nuts, fruits, and vegetables will also be good for your heart as it is low in fat. The fats you use in vegetarian cooking should be vegetable fats and oils such as olive oil, coconut oil or groundnut oil. There is no reason to exclude butter from a vegetarian diet especially if most of the fat you are consuming is of vegetable origin.

One of the great things about a healthful vegetarian diet is that it helps to maintain you weight at the right level. You will still pile on the pounds if you binge on ice cream but a really healthful vegetarian diet leaves you feeling satisfied so that you are less likely to overindulge in sweet things.

Don't Be A Lazy Vegetarian

Vegetarianism has become big business. The shelves of our supermarkets are full of products aimed at the vegetarian. They all look so convenient and we all need to save time. We are inevitably tempted to be a bit lazy sometimes and cut corners.

But vegetarians need to be aware what is in those handy little packages or they could be putting their health at risk. So don't be a lazy vegetarian in the supermarket: read those labels.

You need to check how much sugar is in the product, how much fat and whether refined carbohydrates have been used. A little bit of refined flour, the occasional sweet or fatty treat are not in themselves bad for a vegetarian. But these substances become a problem when they make up a large part of the vegetarian diet.

Even a vegetarian can get fat if they eat enough fat, sugar and refined carbohydrate. As a vegetarian, you should train your palate and that of your children to expect less of these foods and the instant sugar rush that goes with them.

Many of the fats used in commercial vegetarian foods are what is called transfatty acids. These are associated with an elevated risk of cancer. So even if the fats used in a vegetarian product are derived from vegetable sources they may have been modified so much in the manufacturing process that they are no longer healthy.

Of course, vegetarians lead busy lives and there are times when we need a quick snack or a meal in hurry. In these situations opt for healthy alternative. A bowl of whole meal cereal will fill that hungry gap before the evening meal when you come home. Keep a good range of fresh fruits on hand. This is natural grab and go vegetarian food.

Vegetarian food does not always take a long time to cook and prepare. Red split lentils take 10 minutes to cook and can become the basis of all kinds of curries, soups, stews and burgers

If you keep some cooked pulse on hand in the fridge you can rustle up a vegetarian meal very quickly. Or cook twice as much as you need when you have the time and freeze it for later. A little planning allows a vegetarian to be lazy in a healthy way.

May be when you feel that vegetarian cooking it just too slow you should ask yourself "What's the hurry?" Vegetarian food should not be a quick refueling stop. Set out a platter of vegetable sticks and olives with a hummous dip. Cut up a loaf of whole meal bread. Take time to discuss the events of the day. By the time you have done that your main vegetarian meal of the evening will be ready.

Alternative Sources Of Protein For The Vegetarian

In a conventional diet protein is obtained from meat, fish, eggs, milk and dairy products such as cheese. These all contain complete proteins that contain all the essential amino acids that are needed for the human body. A vegetarian diet must derive protein from other sources.

Protein is found in many vegetable sources. Some of these vegetable proteins are complete in that they contain all the essential amino acids just like animal protein. Others are incomplete and must be combined together to produce a complete protein that the body can use.

Most plant foods contain some protein. A vegetarian who eats a wide variety of foods will consume sufficient protein in the course of day.

Nuts and seeds are an under appreciated source of protein. They can be added to a wide range of sweet and savory vegetarian dishes.

Soya beans are source of complete protein and for that reason soya products are an important part of a vegetarian diet. Commercially manufactured soya based meat substitutes are now widely available in supermarkets. They come in variety of forms and are often made into pies, burgers, sausages and other ready prepared products that offer the busy vegetarian a convenience food.

Soya milk can be found in most chiller cabinets next to the cows' milk. You will also find soya yoghurts and soya cheeses. A more traditional soya product is tofu which has long been used in Chinese cooking.

Another meat substitute is mycoprotein which is made from a variety of fungus. Like soya protein it is sold in various forms that can be used in a range of recipes. You will also find it in ready made products often sold under the brand name "Quorn."

Beans, peas and lentils, known collectively as pulse, make up one of the major sources of protein for a vegetarian. They are incomplete proteins and must be combined with other incomplete proteins, such as grains, or complete proteins, such as eggs or milk, to make a complete protein food. Usually this is done in one dish such as beans and rice or beans on toast, but this is not always necessary as the body can store protein and combine it later.

Three Health Advantages Of A Vegetarian Diet

A vegetarian diet offers a number of health advantages when compared to the typical diet that is eaten by the majority of people in the rich industrial countries. The healthy character of a vegetarian diet derives from the fact that it is rich in fruit and vegetables, contains large amounts of fibre and is low in animal fat.

In recent years the problems of heart disease, obesity, diabetes, the degenerative diseases of old age and cancers have been on the increase. Provided it is well planned, a vegetarian diet addresses all the modern health problems.

It is possible to become obese on a vegetarian diet, but an overweight vegetarian is a rarity. A vegetarian diet is likely to include many slow release carbohydrates, such as brown rice, whole meal bread and root vegetables, that raise the body's blood sugar level slowly. This has major implications for both obesity and type 2 diabetes.

Much of the fat in a vegetarian diet is derived from nuts and seeds which contain essential fatty acids known as omega 3, 6 and 9. These essential fatty acids do not raise cholesterol levels and so benefit the heart. They play a vital role in the brain and help to maintain the suppleness of joints, as well as ensuring good skin and hair.

Soya products make up an important component of a vegetarian diet. Studies show that soya actively reduced the body's cholesterol levels and so contributes to heart health.

One of the key health advantages of a vegetarian diet is its high fibre content. Fruit, vegetables and whole grains all contain fibre. Fibre is essential to maintain the health of the colon and bowels. Studies have shown that a high fibre diet is linked to a low incidence of pre-cancerous growths in the colon.

The fruit and vegetables that a vegetarian consumes contain important anti-oxidants which combat the free radicals that can cause cancer.

The Top Five Nutrients Vegetarians Lack

When you are beginning the process of converting to a vegetarian diet it is important to plan carefully. You need to make yourself familiar with the nutrient value of your food and how foods interact with one another.

A vegetarian diet can be lacking in five essential nutrients unless it is planned. These are protein, iron. calcium, zinc and vitamin B-12. In a meat based diet these are easily obtained from animal products. If dairy produce and eggs are included in a vegetarian diet these essential nutrients should not be in short supply.

If you have decided to eat a vegetarian diet, whether for reasons of health or because of ethical considerations, you need to consider where you will obtain these nutrients. It is perfectly possible for a vegetarian to derive these nutrients from vegetable sources with a little thought.

A vegetarian can obtain protein from beans, peas, lentils and other pulses. These vegetarian staples need to be mixed with grains such as rice, barley or wheat, which also contain protein, because only together do they make what is called a complete protein. A complete protein contains all the essential amino acid that are found in meat and other animal products.

Soya beans are unique among beans in containing all the essential amino acids without the addition of grains. Soya products make up an important part of a vegetarian diet for that reason. Soya milk, soya yoghurt, soya cheeses, tofu and soya meat substitutes make up an important part of a healthy vegetarian diet.

A vegetarian diet need not be lacking in protein if it contains a variety of pulse, grains, nuts and seeds. Sprinkling a few sesame seeds on a meal will increase its protein content.

It is not even necessary to include different incomplete vegetable proteins in the same meal to create a balanced protein. The body is capable of storing amino acids and combining them later.

Many of the commercially available soya products have calcium, zinc and vitamin B-12 added in the manufacturing process. But a vegetarian should also ensure that these nutrients are present in the rest of their diet.

Soya beans are also a good source of iron as are seeds such as pumpkin seeds. Quinoa, a seed that cooks like rice and can be used as the starch component of a meal contains iron.

Zinc is vital for growth and cell division. It is essential for reproductive health. for liver function and insulin activity. It is present in dairy foods as well as beans, lentils nuts and seeds. Chick peas are a good source of zinc, as is tahini paste. A hummous dip is more than a tasty snack it is valuable source of a nutrients in a vegetarian diet.

Calcium need not be a major problem in a vegetarian diet. If a vegetarian diet includes dairy produce it will provide enough calcium. Even for vegans it is possible to obtain calcium from plant sources. Whole meal bread is a fairly good source of calcium as are dried apricots. Baked beans and broccoli are both good sources of calcium.

Where vitamin B-12 is concerned it is only necessary to resort to supplements if eggs and milk are excluded from a vegetarian diet.

Ideas For Adding Some Variety To Your Vegetarian Lifestyle

Variety is not only good for vegetarians because the same old food can become boring but it is also necessary. Making sure that your vegetarian diet is varied is the best way to ensure that your get enough of the right nutrients.

You should never stick to one or two recipes and never be tempted to confine yourself to a few commercial products because they seem easy to prepare. If you do that you simply will not get a balanced diet and you will become bored. That is why so many vegetarians give up after a short time.

When you visit the supermarket spend time in the fresh produce section. If your usual store does not carry fresh produce go to another one or find a local supplier. Fresh fruit and vegetables are the main stay of a healthy and varied vegetarian diet.

Get to know what is in season and how to prepare it. A vegetarian should learn what fresh fruit and vegetables look like, feel like and smell like. Vegetarians who can shop in farmers' markets have an advantage. But many supermarkets are improving the range of fruit and vegetables they stock.

If you choose a variety of colors of fruit and vegetables you will automatically have a range of nutrients. Vegetarian meals should not be colorless.

The look of food is often underestimated by vegetarians. But we eat with our eyes. The sight of a plate of beautiful food sets out mouth salivating as much as the smell of new baked bread.

Speaking of new baked bread, vegetarians should learn to bake bread. A sourdough rye loaf fresh from the oven or a crusty whole meal with poppy seeds can make a simple vegetarian meal into a gourmet feast. A simple vegetarian sold or a bowl of lentil can become a complete meal with good bread.

If eating butter is a problem because you are watching your cholesterol levels then dip your bread in olive oil. When you try this with quality home made bread you will see how delicious it is. Vegetarians have respect for vegetables so find the best olive you can. It will be worth it. The varied taste of olive oil from different countries or even different estates will in itself add variety to you vegetarian diet.

Beans, lentils and grains are the staples of vegetarian diet. But they can become boring. Never be afraid to try new types or pulse and grain. if you have never eaten quinoa then you should. It is quick to cook and makes a change from rice. Try using barley instead of rice. Even the vegetarian staples need not be dull.

Making A Vegan Cake

Making a cake for a vegan sounds like a daunting task and possibly not be very rewarding one. No eggs, no butter, and no milk - how can that be a cake. But the secret is to stop thinking of it as a series of prohibitions and think of it as an opportunity to be creative.

Your vegan cake may be the best one you have ever made if you think outside the box. You are not making a substitute for a traditional cake. You are making a vegan cake. This is a cake in its own right.

A vegan cake might be a stack of pancakes made with buckwheat flour and layered with cashew cream and fresh strawberries. Cashew cream is made by grinding cashew nuts with a small quantity of water in a food processor.

Many fruit cakes do not require eggs because they are not intended to rise very high like a sponge cake. When decorated with icing they will be indistinguishable from any other fruit cake. Obviously you must use vegetable margarine.

A brownie type cake can be made without egg using only baking powder to make it rise. It will not have the height of a traditional sponge cake. But once it is cool you can assemble it into a taller and more impressive creation.

A cake of this kind can be made with good quality vegetable oil rather than margarine. This has definite health benefits.

For preference use whole meal flour in your vegan cake. You can also cut down on sugar or eliminate it altogether by using applesauce or grated carrot to sweeten it. This will make your vegan cake a much healthier option.

Sometimes you will have just have to make a birthday cake. In this case you will have to resort to an egg substitute. There is no other way to get the effect of a sponge that rises and stays risen when baked. The protein in the egg sets in the process of baking. Your local health food store will be able to provide you with a product known as Ener-G Egg Replacer. This will do the job and allow you to produce a vegan cake that is indistinguishable from a the "real thing."

Why Vegans Don't Consume Dairy Products

Becoming a vegan means giving up milk and dairy products such as butter and cheese. This a major change for people who are used to a European diet that historically has always used dairy produce.

But in many cultures dairy produce is eaten at all or only rarely. A vegan diet is common in some non-Western societies. It is therefore entirely possible to eat a balanced vegan diet that does not include dairy produce.

The emphasis on dairy produce in the Western diet has produced an enormous industry to stock our supermarket shelves. The nature of this industry is perhaps one of the best reasons for becoming a vegan and cutting milk and dairy produce out of your diet.

What was once a treat for high days and holidays has become a daily staple. There are powerful commercial interests involved in encouraging us to eat more dairy produce. That change in our diet has had serious effects on health. The same changes can be seen in other cultures that are in the process of changing to a Western diet.

The demand for milk has created an intensive dairy industry in which cows are treated as units of production not living creatures. Dairy cows are selectively bred for the highest milk yield. They are impregnated every year so that they continue to produce milk.

Cows in intensive dairy units are treated with antibiotics and hormones. Some of them never set foot on grass. The old image of the placid dairy cow in a green field is a thing of the past.

Calves are no more than a by-product of the process of producing milk. They are taken from their mothers within weeks of their birth. Male calves are disposed of as uneconomic or are sent for veal production.

More humane farming systems are used on some farms. Vegetarians who wish to consume dairy produce should seek out milk produced on farms with high welfare standards.

But even if you can source good quality dairy produce from farms with high welfare standards you may wish to eliminate dairy produce from your diet and become a vegan. A vegan diet is a realistic option and for many people a vegan diet is an ethical option.

Why Vegans Don't Eat Eggs

Vegans are vegetarians who do not eat eggs or any other animal product. This is the strictest form of vegetarianism.

Many people feel that this is too extreme and too restrictive. They prefer a form of vegetarianism that includes eggs and other animal products that do not involve the death or harm of living creatures.

Vegetarians cooking for children are often advised to include some eggs in their diet. Pregnant women who are vegetarians often do the same. The advantage of eggs is that they are highly nutritious. They contain the same nutrients as meat because they are the food supply for the embryonic chick.

But modern farming techniques are convincing an increasing number of people that it is unethical to eat eggs. The battery farms in which most of the eggs available on supermarket shelves are produced cause harm and suffering to millions of hens. They are kept in confined conditions without space to move and engage in natural behavior. As a result they peck one another and have to be de-beaked. Their legs are malformed and they lose their feathers.

Some of us opt for free range eggs but there is no agreed definition of what free range means. Without visiting the farm it is very hard to know how the hens that produced the eggs have been treated. Even in a free range setting the chicks have been selected to ensure that they are female. A huge number of male chicks are discarded in this process and go into industrially prepared foods.

You might decide to raise your own hens. Backyard poultry keeping is becoming increasingly popular. But even here there are ethical decisions to be made. Hens that are no longer laying eggs traditionally go into the pot. That is fine if you are a carnivore but not if you are a vegetarian.

There are also strong health reasons for not eating eggs. Eggs are a source of saturated fat. They can raise you cholesterol level. So if you are worried about your heart health and have been told to reduce you cholesterol level it may be worth thinking about a vegan diet. It is possible for an adult to eat a balanced diet that does not include eggs.

You Are What You Eat

You've certainly heard the expression many times, "You are what you eat." Have you ever really thought about what it means? And do you think about it when you're making food choices?

In some ways, we do become what we eat, literally. Have you ever seen an example of your blood plasma after eating a fast food hamburger? What was previously a clear liquid becomes cloudy with the fat and cholesterol that's absorbed from eating a high-fat hamburger.

And when you think about it, we also become what we don't eat. When we switch from eating meat to a vegetarian-based diet, we become less fat, less prone to many types of cancers. Our cholesterol can improve. When we're leaner and eating fewer animal products, then many other health and fitness issues are reduced. The incidence of Type II diabetes is reduced. Blood pressure falls into normal ranges. When you're healthier, you're taking fewer medications. Even if you have a prescription drug benefit in your health plan, you're still saving money with fewer co-payments on medications.

If you have a family history of high cholesterol or high blood pressure, then it's particularly incumbent on you to revise your eating habits. Moving towards a more vegetarian diet has been shown statistically to reduce the incidence of so many of the diseases of industrialized countries. Vegetarians are statistically healthier than omnivorous persons; they're leaner and live longer.

Isn't it time to think about what you want to be and to eat accordingly? Do you want to be sluggish and fat? Do you want the risk that goes with eating animal products, with their high fat content? Or do you want to look like and be what vegetarians are? Leaner and fitter with a longer anticipated lifespan. It's never too late to change what you're doing and increase your chances for a longer, fitter life.

Turkeys

The consumption of turkeys in the U.S. has escalated through the years. It's no longer eaten primarily at Thanksgiving and Christmas, but throughout the year. The process of mass-producing turkeys for human consumption is as barbaric, if not more so, than the process of mass-producing chickens.

Turkeys are kept in cramped, dark spaces to discourage the naturally aggressive behaviors that occur when an animal is kept confined without space to roam and feed freely. They're overfed to the point where their legs can't support the weight of the breast tissue. And this animal which normally has a 10-years life span is generally slaughtered at about 2 years of age.

Unhealthy and overcrowded conditions mean that disease amongst commercial turkeys is widespread, resulting in approximately 2.7 million turkeys dying in their sheds every year. Foot and leg deformities, heat stress and starvation caused by the inability of immature birds to find the feed and water troughs are commonplace. Ulcerated feet and hock burns are common - caused by continual contact with litter contaminated by urine and feces.

Can you really sit at dinner on your next holiday and look at a roasted turkey the same way? Turkeys come with the same recommendations for cleanliness and cooking that chickens do. You have to be sure they're cooked to a specific temperature to ensure that any disease-causing bacteria are completely killed. You should clean up any counter space with bleach, again to kill all bacteria.

It makes a compelling case for switching to a vegetarian diet, doesn't it? Suddenly, the jokes about vegetarian dinners, with nut loaves and vegetables, instead of meat, seem to make more sense, not only from a health standpoint, but from a humane issue as well. Why do we persist in eating in such a way that makes us unhealthy and is inherently bad for us? For you next holiday dinner, consider the possibilities of an all-vegetarian menu. So much of the dinner is vegetable-based to begin with; it's a small change to replace turkey with a plant-based main course as well.

Pig Farming

Many people reject eating pork and other meats derived from pigs for religious reasons or health reasons. When people start eating a more vegetarian diet, red meat is usually the first thing they eliminate from their diets. When they do, various health indicators generally start to improve, such as their cholesterol levels and blood pressure readings. Health is one of the most compelling reasons to eat vegetarian, but the inhumane treatment of the animals mass-produced for human consumption is another reason many people are rejecting a carnivorous diet.

Pig farming follows the same processes that chicken farming and other animal farming employ. The pigs are kept in small crates with limited movement. They're overfed so they can be slaughtered more quickly. Their living conditions can be dirty and they're fed growth hormones to stimulate weight gain and antibiotics to ward off diseases that are the results of their living conditions.

They're forced to live in unnatural conditions and they exhibit signs of chronic stress that other animals produced for human food do. They chew on the bars of their cages or worry with their water bottles excessively. Their limited range of movement prevents the rooting behavior that's natural for a pig.

The pigs pay an extremely high price to feed us. And we pay a high price for eating pork and other red meat. We're basically not made to eat meat. Our teeth weren't developed to rip and tear meat. We evolved from herbivores and it's still the better way for us to eat. When we eliminate red meat and other meats and animal products from our diet, we get healthier – more lean and fit, less tired and sluggish. And there's the added psychological benefit of knowing that we're not contributing to the suffering of innocent animals.

Fish, Mercury

Many people think if they just eliminate red meat and poultry from their diets, their eating healthier. This is partly true, but there are hazards to eating fish and seafood as well. The harm that humans have done to the environment has had a direct effect on the fish and seafood we eat.

There are elements of fish and shellfish are an important part of a healthy diet. Fish and shellfish contain high-quality protein and other essential nutrients, are low in saturated fat, and contain omega-3 fatty acids. A well-balanced diet that includes a variety of fish and shellfish can contribute to heart health and children's proper growth and development. So, women and young children in particular should include fish or shellfish in their diets due to the many nutritional benef its.

However, nearly all fish and shellfish contain traces of mercury. For most people, the risk from mercury by eating fish and shellfish is not a health concern. Yet, some fish and shellfish contain higher levels of mercury that may harm an unborn baby or young child's developing nervous system. The risks from mercury in fish and shellfish depend on the amount of fish and shellfish eaten and the levels of mercury in the fish and shellfish. Therefore, the Food and Drug Administration (FDA) and the Environmental Protection Agency (EPA) are advising women who may become pregnant, pregnant women, nursing mothers, and young children to avoid some types of fish and eat fish and shellfish that are lower in mercury.

Is this anyway to eat? In fear of what unhealthy elements are lurking in the food we eat? Eliminating red meat and eating a more vegetarian diet is an excellent start on the road to more healthy eating. Eliminating fish and seafood is one of the final steps towards eating a complete vegetarian diet and the health benefits that are your reward for making that change.

<u>Animal Suffering</u>

What are the reasons we eat food? That might seem like a silly question, because we eat to feed our bodies, first of all. Many of us also obtain an emotional gratification when we eat, and most of us are omnivores, meaning we eat everything, including meat and poultry.

There are many compelling reasons to move towards a vegetarian diet, many of them health-related. But many people refuse to eat meat because of the inhumane treatment of the animals that are mass-produced to feed the population. Animal farming on the scale that it needs to be to satisfy U.S. consumption is grotesquely cruel. When you eat meat, you're eating the flesh of an animal whose life has been artificially shortened by overfeeding it to get it to a slaughterhouse earlier. They're kept in small pens and cages, where they endure chronic stress. If they bear their young live, their babies are taken from them, sometimes a day after they're born. They're fed growth hormones and antibiotics and kept from the natural behaviors and actions that characterize the normal life span. Pigs aren't allowed to root. Calves are kept immobile. Chickens are kept in cages, their beaks seared off with a burning hot knife to thwart aggressive behaviors that are the result of unnatural confinement.

Do you really think the flesh of the animal is separate from its spirit and its energy? The agony and stress they endure in their shortened lives infuses every cell of their bodies. Consider that depression and stress can make humans ill, can infect our muscles and organs. Is an animal so very different? We don't need meat or milk for survival. We're no longer a hunting society; we're merely a consuming society.

Isn't it time we all started thinking differently of what we consume to nourish our bodies? We're evolved from herbivores, and yet we've veered off our own evolutionary path. One can make a case for hunting and eating meat when it's the only means for survival. But that's no longer the case and our options are plentiful. Do they have to include the flesh of suffering animals? How can that possibly be considered nourishment?

Different Types Of Vegetarians

Many people think of vegetarians as one homogeneous group that just doesn't eat meat. But nothing could be further from the truth. There are different categories of vegetarians as diverse as the reasons for going vegetarian in the first place.

A vegetarian is generally defined as someone who doesn't eat meat. But someone who is vegetarian could conceivably eat dairy products such as milk, eggs and cheese. A lacto ovo vegetarian doesn't eat meat, fish or poultry, but does consume eggs, milk or cheese. A lacto vegetarian consumes milk and cheese products, but doesn't consume eggs.

A vegan is someone who doesn't consume any animal product or by-product, including dairy food. They eat only vegetables, fruits, nuts, grains and legumes. They also don't use animal products, such as leather. Vegans also don't use white sugar because it's often processed with a substance derived from animal bones that whitens the sugar.

There are other categories within the vegetarian community. Fruitarians, for example, eat only fruit. Their rationale is that fruits, including fruits such as tomatoes, are self-perpetuating and don't need to be planted to create the food source. They consider it a way of eating that's most in balance and harmony with the earth, the most natural.

All of the above will eat cooked vegetables, fruits and legumes. There is also a growing movement towards eating only raw or living foods. This based on the assumption that cooking food processes most of the nutrients out of it, and to get all the nutritional value, vitamins and amino acids from food, it's best consumed raw, or juiced. If cooked at all, it should only be cooked to slightly over 100 degrees, so the nutrients are still retained.

The more restrictive you become with your diet, however, the more educated you need to become to be sure you're getting all the necessary proteins and vitamins that you need to maintain good health, especially muscle and heart health.

Vegetarians And Heart Disease

No matter what your reasons for eating a more vegetarian diet, there's no denying the obvious health benefits that are derived from the elimination of red meat from your diet. On average, vegetarians have lower levels of the blood fats, cholesterol and triglycerides than meat eaters of similar age and social status have. High levels of blood fats are associated with an increased risk of heart disease. Lacto-ovo vegetarians, those who eat eggs and dairy products, which contain cholesterol-raising saturated fats and cholesterol, have higher cholesterol levels than do vegans, as those who abstain from all animal foods are called. But even among lacto-ovo vegetarians, cholesterol levels are generally lower than they are among meat eaters.

Researchers have found that older men who eat meat six or more times a week are twice as likely to die of heart disease as those who abstain from meat. Among middle-aged men, meat eaters were four times more likely to suffer a fatal heart attack, according to the study. As for women, who are partly protected by their hormones and generally develop heart disease later in life than men do, the risk of fatal heart disease has been found to be lower only among the older vegetarians. In a 1982 study of more than 10,000 vegetarians and meat eaters, British researchers found that the more meat consumed, the greater the risk of suffering a heart attack. Though eliminating meat from the diet is likely to reduce your consumption of heart-damaging fats and cholesterol, substituting large amounts of high-fat dairy products and cholesterol-rich eggs can negate the benefit. To glean the heart-saving benefits of vegetarianism, consumption of such foods as hard cheese, cream cheese, ice cream and eggs should be moderate. And the introduction of more vegetables, fruits and raw foods will definitely enhance the benefits of abstaining from eating meat.

Vegetarians And Cancer

You might have a general idea that eating a vegetarian diet is more healthy for you. But do you really know how much less the incidence is of certain types of cancers among vegetarians?

Vegetarian diets—naturally low in saturated fat, high in fiber, and replete with cancer-protective phytochemicals—help to prevent cancer. Large studies in England and Germany have shown that vegetarians are about 40 percent less likely to develop cancer compared to meat-eaters. In the U.S., studies of Seventh-Day Adventists, who are largely lacto-ovo vegetarians, have shown significant reductions in cancer risk among those who avoided meat. Similarly, breast cancer rates are dramatically lower in nations, such as China, that follow plant-based diets. Interestingly, Japanese women who follow Western-style, meat-based diets are eight times more likely to develop breast cancer than women who follow a more traditional plant-based diet. Meat and dairy products contribute to many forms of cancer, including cancer of the colon, breast, ovaries, and prostate.

Harvard studies that included tens of thousands of women and men have shown that regular meat consumption increases colon cancer risk by roughly 300 percent. High-fat diets also encourage the body's production of estrogens. Increased levels of this sex hormone have been linked to breast cancer. A recent report noted that the rate of breast cancer among premenopausal women who ate the most animal (but not vegetable) fat was one-third higher than that of women who ate the least animal fat. A separate study from Cambridge University also linked diets high in saturated fat to breast cancer. One study linked dairy products to an increased risk of ovarian cancer. The process of breaking down the lactose (milk sugar) evidently damages the ovaries. Daily meat consumption triples the risk of prostate enlargement. Regular milk consumption doubles the risk and failure to consume vegetables regularly nearly quadruples the risk.

Vegetarians avoid the animal fat linked to cancer and get abundant fiber, vitamins, and phytochemicals that help to prevent cancer. In addition, blood analysis of vegetarians reveals a higher level of "natural killer cells," specialized white blood cells that attack cancer cells.

Bowels And Stomach Digestion

Many of the health benefits derived from a vegetarian diet have to do with creating a healthy environment in the bowels and stomach. Our digestive systems, from prehistory on, were designed to metabolize vegetable matter, more than animal products. Fruits, vegetables, legumes and nuts provide the kind of dietary fiber our digestive systems need to function properly. The Western diet that's high in processed and refined flour and sugar, and in animal products that are laden with hormones and antibiotics, are actually anathema to our insides.

When the digestive system doesn't function and work as it's intended to, that leads to opportunistic diseases or changes in the DNA of cells in the stomach and colon. And there are more practical considerations as well. When we don't get enough of the fiber we need, we incur a host of digestion and elimination problems, such as constipation and hemorrhoids that are a result of straining. These diseases and syndromes are much less evident in a vegetarian population than in a meat-eating population.

Other diseases of the bowel that occur less frequently in a vegetarian population include irritable bowel syndrome, and chronic ulcerative colitis, mostly likely due to the increased fiber content in a vegetarian diet. And of course a diet that's higher in dietary fiber that comes from a vegetarian diet will decrease the likelihood or risk of colon cancer.

When you consider the risks that come with a diet that includes meat and animal products, and the benefits that come from a vegetarian diet, does the prospect of a steak or burger or bacon really sound that good to you? Doesn't it at least make sense to reverse the portion sizes and proportions of meats to vegetables and side dishes? In other words, if you must continue to eat meat, then make meat your side dish, or just incidental to your meal, such as in a stir fry. Increasing the proportion of fruits and vegetables in your diet can only be good for you.

Weight

Think about it, have you ever seen a fat vegetarian? Probably not. In fact, for most of us, vegetarian is almost synonymous with lean and healthy, isn't it? And when you start any diet, what's the first thing the experts tell you? Generally it's to increase the amounts of vegetables you're eating and to eat limited amounts of meat, especially high-fat red meat and pork.

And what happens when you resume your old eating habits? Generally the weight will come right back on. Even the greatest will-power can't overcome the unhealthy effects of eating high-fat meat.

When you eat a diet that's higher in dietary fiber, that's primarily if not totally vegetarian, you're naturally healthier. You're feeding your body and getting it the nutrition it needs to run efficiently. You have more energy and stamina; you wake up more easily and more refreshed. It's easier to exercise, because you're not so weighed down by digesting the high fat and excessive protein that comes from eating a carnivorous diet.

Many diets fail because we think of them as depriving ourselves of food we love. The trick is to change that thinking. There are so many compelling reasons to eliminate meat from our diet, so why not forget about losing weight? Focus instead on eating healthier, or eating in a way that's in balance with the earth, and that doesn't need to subsist on the suffering of animals. You'll probably find you'll start to lose weight without even thinking about it!

And when you do lose weight, so many other health risks can fall by the wayside as well. You'll find your blood pressure falls into a healthier range and your risk for Type II diabetes can decrease. You'll look better and feel better and probably never go back to your old ways of eating!

Osteoporosis

You know that eating a vegetarian diet can decrease the incidence of heart disease and certain types of cancers. You also know that it can make you leaner and healthier. But so many of the health studies are done on men? What about women and the impact of a vegetarian diet on their health as they age?

Diets that are high in protein, especially animal protein, tend to cause the body to excrete more calcium, oxalate, and uric acid. These three substances are the main components of urinary tract stones. British researchers have advised that persons with a tendency to form kidney stones should follow a vegetarian diet. The American Academy of Family Physicians notes that high animal protein intake is largely responsible for the high prevalence of kidney stones in the United States and other developed countries and recommends protein restriction for the prevention of recurrent kidney stones.

For many of the same reasons, vegetarians are at a lower risk for osteoporosis. Since animal products force calcium out of the body, eating meat can promote bone loss. In nations with mainly vegetable diets (and without dairy product consumption), osteoporosis is less common than in the U.S., even when calcium intake is also less than in the U.S. Calcium is important, but there is no need to get calcium from dairy products.

We continue to consume meat, while at the same time downing calcium supplements and prescription drugs to prevent osteoporosis, that often have drastic side effects. And most experts agree that calcium supplements are inferior to calcium derived from natural food sources. Doesn't it make more sense (and cents) to get your calcium from eating a healthier diet?

What are some good vegetarian sources of calcium? Orange juice, for one. Dry beans, such as black-eyed peas, kidney beans and black beans are another good source, as are dark leafy vegetables such as broccoli and kale. Tofu is also a good source of calcium.

Humans Did Not Always Eat Meat

Do you ever think about how far we've diverted from the path of our pre-historic ancestors and they're eating patterns? Consider how the earliest humans evolved, and what they ate. They were hunter-gatherers and did not evolve with the characteristics of carnivores. Humans aren't made to tear animals apart and eat their flesh. When you look at carnivorous animals, such as wild cats, you can see their teeth are designed to rip and tear, not chew.

Humans evolved from vegetarian creatures. Even our digestive systems are not particularly suited to eating meat. Eating meat is a relatively recent development in human history, most likely born of opportunity and necessity. Perhaps earliest man observed carnivores eating meat, and if they couldn't find any of the natural foods they were used to eating, such as vegetables, berries, nuts and grains, then they might have assumed that eating meat would at least sustain lif e.

But initially we emulated the creatures we evolved from, herbivores like apes. Even to a prehistoric mind, apes would have looked similar to man, walking primarily upright, with arms and hands. We naturally would have foraged for our food, eating roots and berries, fruits and nuts. We would have watched the apes peeling bananas, or crushing nuts on stones to get at the meat of the nut.

We would have been living more moment-to-moment, constantly foraging for food. Hunting, after all, requires thought and planning. Eating meat requires preparation and most importantly, fire. Until man discovered fire, he was primarily vegetarian, living in what was the natural order of things. Vegetarian eating is a more natural way of eating, in addition to being healthier. It's a way that's in balance with the planet, and doesn't seek to dominate it and conquer it.

Spirituality

How do you feel spiritually when you eat a meal that contains meat? You've probably never given it any thought, but that may because spiritually you feel nothing after eating a meal of meat except tired and sluggish. A diet of meat makes our bodies less functional, and we think of nourishing our bodies in terms of our organs and blood, but we don't often think about how what we eat can impact the most important organ in our body, the brain.

When you eat a vegetarian diet, you begin to feel physically lighter and fit. When your body is fit, your mind is also lightened. Most cultures that focus more on spirituality and enlightenment are also vegetarian cultures. From the beginning of recorded history we can see that vegetables have been the natural food of human beings. Early Greek and Hebrew myths all spoke of people originally eating fruit. Ancient Egyptian priests never ate meat. Many great Greek philosophers such as Plato, Diogenes, and Socrates all advocated vegetarianism.

In India, Shakyamuni Buddha emphasized the importance of Ahimsa, the principle of not harming any living things. He warned His disciples not to eat meat, or else other living beings would become frightened of them. Buddha made the following observations: "Meat eating is just an acquired habit. In the beginning we were not born with a desire for it." "Flesh eating people cut off their inner seed of Great Mercy." "Flesh eating people kill each other and eat each other ... this life I eat you, and next life you eat me ... and it always continues in this way. How can they ever get out of the Three Realms (of illusion)?"

These are cultures that are considered more enlightened and focused more on spirituality than is Western culture. If we are to evolve into more spiritual beings, then we must begin to manage our physical lives in a way that will enhance our spirituality, and this means taking the path of vegetarianism as a path to enlightenment.

Transition Family

If you're considering moving to a vegetarian diet as an adult, you probably want to pass on this good nutrition and improved way of eating to your family as well. In fact, it's your responsibility as a parent to nurture your children and help them develop physically, mentally and spiritually.

But that can be hard to do, especially in a culture where our children are bombarded with messages from fast food restaurants in the media. How do you teach kids to resist the siren song of Ronald McDonald? There isn't a plate of vegetables on the planet that's going to look as good to them as a Happy Meal!

You have to start slowly to change not only your own eating patterns, but your family's as well. Like any other dietary endeavor, it starts at the grocery store. Begin stocking the refrigerator with healthy snacks like apples and carrots. Exchange good, chewy brown rice for white rice and processed side dishes, which are so high in fat and sodium. Make meat portions smaller and smaller and start incorporating more vegetables and grains in your family dinners.

Don't make changes all at once. If you do give in and stop at a fast food restaurant, get fruit or yogurt in addition to or part of that meal. Make the changes so gradual that they'll never notice their diets are changing. Kids are usually very sympathetic about animals, and it's not too early to talk to them about eating in a way that isn't cruel to animals.

You'll be doing them a favor that will last them a lifetime. With childhood obesity at epidemic levels in the U.S., you will be setting up your children for lifelong eating habits that will help ensure a long and healthy life.

Detoxification

When people talk about detoxification and cleansing the body of harmful toxins, it's often seen as a fringe element of vegetarians. People really don't like to think about harmful toxins building up in their colons or in their arteries, but it's often a by-product of a carnivorous diet. A diet that's high in fat and processed foods tends to slow down our digestive systems, and our elimination processes are also interrupted.

This can allow harmful bacteria and toxins to accumulate and can create a general feeling of sluggishness, as well as a host of digestive disorders, such as irritable bowel syndrome or colitis. When we begin eating a more healthy vegetarian diet, we start to get more dietary fiber into our systems, and all of a sudden, our digestive systems start to work better,

When you eliminate high-fat meat and processed foods from your diet, then much of your body's energy is freed from the intense work of digesting these foods. Everything becomes clearer – your blood, your organs, your mind. You start to become more aware of the toxic nature of the food you'd been eating before.

Toxicity is of much greater concern in the twentieth century than ever before. There are many new and stronger chemicals, air and water pollution, radiation and nuclear power. We ingest new chemicals, use more drugs of all kinds, eat more sugar and refined foods, and daily abuse ourselves with various stimulants and sedatives. The incidence of many toxicity diseases has increased as well. Cancer and cardiovascular disease are two of the main ones. Arthritis, allergies, obesity, and many skin problems are others. In addition, a wide range of symptoms, such as headaches, fatigue, pains, coughs, gastrointestinal problems, and problems from immune weakness, can all be related to toxicity. When you start a vegetarian eating plan, your body eventually cleanses itself of the harmful effects of these toxic foods.

Eliminate Red Meat

If you're thinking of changing to a vegetarian diet, how do you start? Do you just start shopping in the produce aisle of the grocery store? You might have some anxiety attached to this change as well, and this is understandable.

Try to think of this as adding to your dietary habits, rather than a drastic change. If your diet has consistently included red meat, perhaps you can start substituting other foods for the red meat. Or eliminate the most processed and high-fat meats first, such as bacon and hamburgers. Certainly try to eliminate fast food burgers, which have such a high fat and sodium content. If you think you'll miss the taste of bacon in the morning, try substituting a turkey or vegetable-based bacon substitute. It won't be the same, but you won't be giving up the foods you're used to all at once.

If you've had a health scare and feel the need to change everything at once, make sure you include a lot of variety in the foods you buy as you begin to discover new flavors and textures that you'll like to replace the ones you're used to eating. If you don't need to make a dramatic change all at once, you'll have a much greater chance of long-term success if you take it slow. Reduce the amount of red meat that you eat on a weekly basis, even if it means substituting pasta with marinara sauce for meat just one night a week. Increase the amounts of fruits and vegetables you eat. Start with raw vegetables at night before dinner so you're not so hungry when you get to the main meal. Start reversing the proportions of meat and vegetables and make meat a side dish, with vegetables and grains your main course.

We're creatures of habit and resistant to change. This is why so many diets fail, because we make drastic changes to facilitate dramatic results, quickly. This is a decision and a change you want to make for a lifetime. Make it a natural and gradual change and you can look forward to many more years of healthy living.

Eliminate Poultry

If you haven't been eating a vegetarian diet for years, and want to make the shift, it's best to do so gradually, in stages. A good way to start is to eliminate red meat and substitute fish or poultry for the red meat you've been eating. While it's not eating more vegetarian, you're at least eliminating the biggest offender in disease-enhancing foods, red meat.

After you've successfully eliminated red meat, then start reducing the amount of poultry you eat. While it's not as bad for you as red meat, because it's not as high in fat, it's still meat that's been raised on a farm in terrible, cramped and inhumane conditions. Poultry is so laden with growth hormones and antibiotics that's it's nothing like a chicken or turkey that we might have hunted for food centuries ago. Chickens are raised in horrible conditions, overfed and then slaughtered. In the grand scheme of things, it's just as detrimental to our physical and spiritual health as eating red meat. It's also fairly easy to eliminate poultry from our diets because let's face it – it's like eating wood pulp, it's so tasteless. All the antibiotics and abnormal living conditions have processed any natural flavor that poultry ever had in the first place.

Add more fish and seafood, if you're not quite ready to replace poultry with grains and vegetables and legumes yet. While there is risk in eating fish and seafood, because of the high levels of mercury they contain, it's a better alternative to poultry and red meat. This may be as far as you ever get in moving towards vegetarianism, or at least eliminating meat from your diet. Give yourself time to get used to this. You won't miss poultry for a minute. We usually eat chicken and chicken breasts because it's lower in fat and calories, but it's also lower in any kind of nutritional value. When we're not getting essential proteins and vitamins, we're still starving our bodies, regardless of how healthy we think we're being. Eliminating poultry is one of the most positive steps you can take towards a healthy diet and a healthy planet.

Eliminate Seafood

It's actually pretty easy to eliminate red meat and poultry from our diets. When you give any thought whatsoever, the reasons are so compelling to stop eating them. Your reasons may be physical, because you need to lower your cholesterol or blood pressure. You may want to reduce your risk of cancers that may run in your family, and eliminating red meat from your diet is an important way to do this. You may also find that the way we mass-produce meat and poultry for consumption in this country is repugnant to you. If we really thought about the way meat and poultry is raised, we'd never eat the stuff again. We're consuming flesh that's been produced from enormous pain and suffering. Even the smallest life has value on this earth; mass producing these animals to slaughter and eat them degrades their lives and degrades our own in the process of eating them.

It might feel like it's carrying things to far to eliminate something as elemental as a shrimp or a scallop. But think about what we dump into the ocean where this food comes from. All our waste and trash gets hauled into the ocean, if it doesn't go into a landfill. Think of the millions of gallons of oil that have been dumped from oil tanker accidents. Think of the impact that the erosion of the ozone layer in the atmosphere has had on every living thing on the planet. There are toxic levels of mercury in fish and seafood, so much so that if you're a woman contemplating getting pregnant, you most definitely shouldn't eat fish. Your risk of producing a baby with birth defects is extremely high if you do.

It can be hard to let go of fish and seafood, because this has a similar texture to red meat and poultry. It's flesh after all, even though it's marine flesh. It might take longer to eliminate fish and seafood from your diet, but keep at the effort. If you've been realizing the benefits of eating more vegetarian, then it's really a small step to take to eliminate this last piece of animal flesh from your diet. Imagine how good you'll feel about yourself and what you're doing for the planet when make that last step and eliminate all meat and animal products from your diet.

Got Milk? Reasons Not To Grab For The Glass

Many Americans, including some vegetarians, still consume large amounts of dairy products, but here are several strong reasons to eliminate dairy products from your diet. Milk has long been praised as a 'weapon' in the war against osteoporosis, but recent clinical research shows that it actually is associated with a higher fracture risk, and there's been no protective effect of dairy calcium on bone. Increasing your intake of green leafy vegetables and beans, along with exercising have been shown to help strengthen bones and increase their density.

Dairy products are also a significant source of fat and cholesterol in the diet, which can increase your risk for cardiovascular disease. A low-fat vegetarian diet that eliminates dairy products, as well as adequate amounts of exercise, proper stress management and quitting smoking not only will help prevent heart disease, but could also reverse it.

Ovarian, breast, and prostate cancers have been linked to dairy product consumption. According to a recent study by Daniel Cramer, a Harvard doctor, when excessive amounts of dairy products are consumed and the body's enzymes are unable to keep pace with breaking down the lactose; it can build up in the blood and affect a woman's ovaries. Another recent study showed that men who had the highest levels of IGF-I, (insulin-like growth factor) which is found in cow's milk, they were at four times the risk of prostate cancer compared to those men who had the lowest levels of IGF-I.

In addition, milk may not provide a consistent and reliable source of Vitamin D in the diet. Milk samplings have been found to have inconsistent levels of Vitamin D, and some have been found to have as much as 500 times the indicated safe level. Excess Vitamin d in the blood can be toxic and can result in calcium deposits in the body's soft tissues.

Milk proteins, milk sugar, fat, and saturated fat in dairy products may pose health risks for children and lead to the development of chronic diseases such as obesity, diabetes, and formation of plaques in the circulatory system that can lead to heart disease. By choosing to consume a nutrient-dense, healthful diet of grains, fruits, vegetables, legumes, and fortified foods including cereals and juices, you can help meet your body's calcium, potassium, riboflavin, and vitamin D requirements easily and simply, without the added health risks from dairy product consumption.

Flipping The Switch To Vegetarianism

If you've made the commitment to becoming vegetarian yet finding it difficult to make the transition in your diet and your lifestyle, here's some suggestions on how to make the switch a smoother ride.

Start out with committing to be a vegetarian for three days per week for the first couple of weeks. Start substituting ingredients in your favorite dishes to make them truly meatless. Throw in mushrooms to that marinara sauce to take the place of meatballs, or try some textured vegetable protein (TVP) in that lasagna recipe. Making simple replacements in your tried and true recipes can inspire you to stay on the vegetarian track once you see how delicious they can be. Next, commit to five days per week for the next two weeks. Study the natural foods aisle at your local grocer, or make it a point to introduce yourself to the local health foods store. Treat yourself to a few new vegetarian products and try them in your next meal. The internet can be a great source of vegetarian recipes. And don't limit yourself to being vegetarian only at home; most all restaurants offer delicious vegetarian entrees, so be sure to try them. You may even find inspiration for your home cooking by doing so.

Now all that's left to do is add two more days on your week, and you'll be a converted vegetarian all week long! After all, you've been doing it for a month now; you've become a seasoned rookie in the game. Take pride in your accomplishments, because not only have you made positive changes in your lifestyle and eating habits, but for the environment and animals as well. Remember it's not about being perfect; every animal-positive change you make it your diet has a great effect. By rewarding yourself for each vegetarian choice you make, and you'll be motivated to continue in the right direction.

Variety Adds Vitality To Your Vegetarian Meals

Probably one of the most perplexing thoughts a person has when they transition to vegetarianism is keeping their diet filled with a variety of fun, diverse, and nutrient-dense foods. It can sometimes feel like you're cutting many options out since you're no longer consuming meat, and it may seem you're losing even more options if you've also decided to cut dairy and eggs from your diet as well. With a little creativity, planning, and forethought, you might be surprised how much variety you can achieve with your new vegetarian diet – perhaps even more than your meat-eating days!

There are some simple substitutions you can experiment with and use as substitutions in your favorite meat recipes. Tempeh, which is cultured soybeans with a chewy texture; tofu (freezing and then thawing gives tofu a meaty texture; the tofu will turn slightly off white in color); and wheat gluten or seitan (made from wheat and has the texture of meat; available in health food or Oriental stores) are all great items to start with.

Milk and other dairy products can also be easily replaced with vegetarian-friendly items. Try soy milk, soy margarine, and soy yogurts, which can be found in health food or Oriental food stores. You can also make nut milks by blending nuts with water and straining, or rice milks by blending cooked rice with water.

A good way to introduce beans to the diet is to use them instead of meat in favorite dishes, like casseroles and chili. Because of their many health benefits, beans should be eaten often. Some great examples are chickpeas, split peas, haricot, lentils (red, green or brown), and kidney beans.

Many nuts and seeds are available both in and out of the shell, whole, halved, sliced, chopped, raw, or roasted. Cashews, peanuts, walnuts, almonds are some easy-to-find favorites. Sunflower and sesame seeds are excellent choices for spicing up salads and other vegetable dishes.

And don't worry that you'll have to give up your favorite Mexican, Italian, or other favorite dishes now that you're vegetarian. Many of them can still be enjoyed and only require slight variations. Some popular and easily convertible dishes include: pasta with tomato sauce, bean burritos, tacos, tostadas, pizza, baked potatoes, vegetable soups, whole grain bread and muffins, sandwiches, macaroni, stir-fry, all types of salad, veggie burgers with French fries, beans and rice, bagels, breakfast cereals, pancakes, and waffles just to name a few. The freezer sections of most big grocery stores carry an assortment of vegetarian convenience foods such as veggie bacon, burgers, and breakfast sausages.

So get in the kitchen and let your creativity lead the way! You'll probably be pleasantly surprised just how much more variety your diet will have as a result.

Lazy Vegetarians Who Choose the Wrong Carbs Risk Health

We've all been there. We've just come in from a long day at work and the last thing on our minds taking the time to prepare a healthy, nutritionally sound vegetarian meal. But choosing a refined or enriched carbohydrate over the beneficial carbohydrates that a solid, well-balanced vegetarian diet offers defeats the purpose of your decision to live a vegetarian lifestyle, and that's for optimal health. Consuming refined carbohydrates presents different hazards to your health.

The over-consumption of refined carbohydrates and sugars can result in excess insulin in the bloodstream. In the presence of excess insulin, glucose, the blood sugar, is converted to triglycerides and stored in the fat cells of the body.

According to one study, consuming refined grains may also increase your risk of getting stomach cancer. The research found that a high intake of refined grains could increase a patient's risk of stomach cancer.

In addition, refined sugars and carbohydrates have been implicated as a contributing factor in increased gallbladder disease, according to a recent study. It showed a direct link between the amount of sugars eaten and the incidence of gallbladder disease. Another study looked at the role carbohydrates play in the incidence of heart disease. The researchers noted that as carbohydrate consumption increased, so did the level of triglycerides in the blood of the participants. Diets low in fat and high in carbohydrates not only dramatically raised triglyceride levels but significantly reduced levels of HDL, the "good" cholesterol.

And lastly, refined white sugars increase the rate at which your body excretes calcium, which is directly connected to your skeletal health. Simply put, as your sugary and refined carbohydrate intake increases, your bone density decreases.

So don't be lazy! Do your body right and take the time to prepare a nutrient-dense and delicious vegetarian meal. Your body, and your conscience, will thank you for it in the long run.

Why Did Humans Start Eating Meat?

It must have felt unnatural at first, to eat animal flesh. After all, we're not so far removed from animals ourselves. Perhaps it even felt cannibalistic. There might not have been that much intellectual distinction between humans and other animals. When humans were pure vegetarians, they were living in harmony with the earth and with the other creatures co-habiting the planet with them. Their closest animal relatives, apes, were vegetarians. Eating the products of the earth, like plants, grains and fruits that they could gather and eat would have seemed the natural order of things.

But necessity is the mother of invention. Prehistoric men who lived in frozen geographies, or who lived in an area that became devastated by fire, would have eaten anything to survive. Just like the soccer players whose plane crashed in the mountains of Chile, and were forced to eat the flesh of other players who died in the crash, earliest man at some point had to make the choice for survival, and that could have consuming meat for the first time and changing human history – and health – forever.

We can imagine that men first ate meat that had been charred or cooked by virtue of being caught in a natural forest fire. They might have subsequently eaten raw meat, if necessary, but we can also imagine that our earliest digestive systems rebelled against eating raw meat.

Imagine having eaten raw foods and vegetables for eons, and all of a sudden, incorporating meat products into your system. You may have heard friends who were vegetarians tell stories of trying to eat meat and becoming violently ill afterwards.

Biologists will tell you we're really not designed to eat meat, but we adapted to it. However, in the timeline of human history, eating meat is a relatively recent evolutionary development.

Proper Planning Prevents Problems

Special care must be taken when planning a vegetarian diet to ensure proper amounts of nutrients are included daily. Nutrients such as protein, iron, calcium, zinc and vitamins B-12 and D can all be easily incorporated into your vegetarian lifestyle with the proper planning. Here are some guidelines to consider when you are planning your weekly shopping trip and organizing your weekly menu.

Plant proteins alone can provide enough of the essential and non-essential amino acids, as long as sources of dietary protein are varied and caloric intake is high enough to meet energy needs. Whole grains, legumes, vegetables, seeds and nuts all contain both essential and non-essential amino acids. Soy proteins, such as soy milk and tofu, have been shown to be equal to proteins of animal origin.

Vegetarians may have a greater risk of iron deficiency than non-vegetarians. Dried fruits and beans, spinach, and brewer's yeast are all good plant sources of iron.

Vitamin B-12 can be found in some fortified breakfast cereals and soy beverages, some brands of brewer's yeast as well as vitamin supplements. Read the labels of other foods carefully; you might be surprised what food is B-12 fortified.

As a vegetarian, it's essential that you have a reliable source of vitamin D, in your diet. Exposure to ultraviolet (UV) light stimulates your body produce its own vitamin D. Daytime outdoor exercise and working in your garden are both great alternatives for obtaining this important nutrient. Those who don't have the opportunity to get out and soak up the sun might want to consider adding a supplement to their diet.

Recent studies suggest that vegetarians absorb and retain more calcium from foods than their non-vegetarian counterparts. Vegetable greens such as spinach, kale and broccoli, and some legumes and soybean products, are good sources of calcium from plants.

Zinc is imperative for growth and development. Good plant sources include grains, nuts and legumes. However, zinc daily zinc requirements are actually quite low. Take care to select a supplement that contains no more than 15-18 mg zinc.

Vegetarians may have a greater risk of iron deficiency than non-vegetarians. Dried beans, spinach, enriched products, brewer's yeast and dried fruits are all good plant sources of iron. When eaten alongside a fruit or vegetable containing high amounts of vitamin C, your body more willingly absorbs the needed iron, so be sure to team these two vital nutrients up as much as possible when meal planning.

Vegetarian Diet For Optimal Personal And Environmental Health

It's been well documented through the years that vegetarians are healthier than people who eat meat. Vegetarians are less likely to be obese, or to have high blood pressure, diabetes, rheumatoid arthritis, or colon cancer. They are also less likely to die from heart disease. Vegetarians have lower blood pressure even when they eat the same amount of salt as meat eaters and exercise less. Many studies show that vegetarians have less instances of colon cancer, due in large part to the differences in the bacterial flora that is present in the colon.

There are many factors in the vegetarian diet that contribute to better health. Vegetarians consume two to three times as much fiber as do meat-eaters, which has been shown to reduce cholesterol and blood glucose levels, and protect against colon cancer. They also consume more antioxidants, which are found in a wide variety of plant foods and protect cells from oxygen-induced damage and reduce the risk for heart disease, arthritis, cancer, and other diseases.

Vegetarians eat more isoflavones than do meat eaters. These compounds, found mostly in soy foods, are a type of phytochemical. Research shows that isoflavones may reduce the risk for prostate cancer and may improve bone health. Vegetarians also consume much less saturated fat and cholesterol than do meat eaters, resulting in significantly lower levels of blood cholesterol, decreased instances of heart disease and possibly for diabetes and cancer. And, since vegetarians do not eat meat, they are not exposed to heme iron, a type of iron found in meat that may increase the risk of heart disease and cancer.

And lastly, vegetarianism is not only optimally healthy for your body, but your environment and the planet's animals. It allows you to live more harmoniously with the world around you, which improves mental and emotional health accordingly.

The Benefits Of A Vegetarian Diet To Diabetics

Diabetics must choose any food they eat very carefully, as each food choice they make has a profound impact on their overall health on a meal-to-meal basis. Diabetes affects people of all ages, both genders, from all walks of life and backgrounds. Untreated, it can cause wounds to heal slowly, infections take longer to cure, blindness, and kidney failure. Diet is one of the most important ways of controlling diabetes, and a vegetarian lifestyle with its emphasis on low fat, high fiber, and nutrient-rich foods is very complementary.

Affecting more than 30 million people worldwide, this disease inhibits the body from properly processing foods. Usually, most of the food we eat is digested and converted to glucose, a sugar which is carried by the blood to all cells in the body and used for energy. The hormone insulin then helps glucose pass into cells. But diabetics are unable to control the amount of glucose in their blood because the mechanism which converts sugar to energy does not work correctly. Insulin is either absent, present in insufficient quantities or ineffective. As a result glucose builds up in the bloodstream and leads to problems such as weakness, inability to concentrate, loss of co-ordination and blurred vision. If the correct balance of food intake and insulin isn't maintained, a diabetic can also experience blood sugar levels that are too low. If this state continues for a prolonged period of time, it can lead to coma and even death.

Though incurable, diabetes can be successfully controlled through diet and exercise, oral medications, injections of insulin, or a combination. Instead of counting calories diabetics must calculate their total carbohydrate intake so that no less than half their food is made up of complex carbohydrates. Many diabetic vegetarians have discovered that as a result of their meatless diet, they've had to use insulin injections less, which gives them a feeling of power and control over their disease.

Sample Two-Day Diabetic Vegetarian Menu

Though the task of planning out a diabetic vegetarian menu might seem a bit daunting, with a little creativity forethought, it can actually be very simple. Consider the following two-day menu for some ideas and inspiration:

Day one

Breakfast: 1/2 cup melon slices
2 slices French toast (made with soy milk and cooked in vegetable oil with
1/4 cup chopped peaches or apricots
4 ounces enriched soymilk

Morning Snack: 1/2 cup fresh grapes
6 assorted low-fat crackers
Sparkling water

Lunch: 1 cup mushroom barley soup with
2 ounces smoked seitan (A chewy, protein-rich food made from wheat gluten and used as a meat substitute)
1/2 cup green and wax bean salad with
2 teaspoons sesame seeds and
2 Tablespoons reduced-fat salad dressing
8 ounces enriched soymilk

Afternoon Snack: 1/2 cup sugar-free chocolate pudding
(You may create this at home with a sugar-free mix
like Sorbee or Estee and any nondairy milk.)

Dinner: 1 cup chili with lentils with
1/4 cup prepared Textured Vegetable Protein (TVP)
over 1/3 cup white rice
1/2 cup steamed or roasted carrots
1/2 cup fresh pineapple slices

Evening Snack: 1/2 cup pretzels

8 ounces enriched soymilk

<u>Day two</u>

Breakfast: 1/3 cup cranberry juice or

sugar free cranberry juice cocktail

3/4 cup cooked oatmeal with 1/2 banana and

1 teaspoon vegan margarine

8 ounces enriched soymilk

Morning Snack: 3 cups low fat popped popcorn with

2 teaspoons nutritional yeast

1/2 cup orange juice

Lunch: 6" pita stuffed with 2 ounces meat substitute (equivalent to 2 ADA meat exchanges),

lettuce, radishes, and cucumbers

1 cup shredded cabbage with

1-1/2 Tablespoons vegan mayonnaise

8 ounces enriched soymilk

Afternoon Snack: Fruit smoothie made with

8 ounces soymilk, 2 ounces silken tofu, and

1/2 cup frozen or fresh berries, blended together

3 sugar-free ginger snaps

Dinner: Baked eggplant (1/2 cup) with

1/4 cup tomato sauce

1/2 cup black beans with 1/3 cup brown rice

one medium baked apple

Evening Snack: 2 Tablespoons peanut butter on 6 crackers

The Special Needs Of The Pregnant Vegetarian

It's apparent that your nutritional needs increase when you are pregnant. However, you only need approximately 300 more calories than normal during this time, so it's imperative that you make wise food choices and eat nutrient-dense food.

A good start is to ensure that you're eating plenty of protein. Your need for protein increases about 30 percent during pregnancy, but most vegetarian women eat more than enough protein in their regular diets. Soy proteins, beans and legumes are wonderful vegetarian sources of protein.

You need to also step up your calcium intake. Each day you need to be eating at least four servings of calcium-rich foods like broccoli, calcium-fortified soy milk, tofu, and dark green leafy vegetables.

Sunlight stimulates your body to naturally produce vitamin D, and it's probably the easiest way to ensure you get an adequate amount each day. You only need about 20 minutes directly on your face and hands two to three times per week, when the sun is weakest. If you aren't able to get out into the sun, be sure to incorporate vitamin-D rich foods into your daily diet by choosing fortified cereals, or using a supplement.

Take a look at your iron intake, as it's a vital mineral during your pregnancy, especially the last half. Choose beans, dark green leafy vegetables, nuts and seeds, or fortified breads and cereals. You might also want to consider supplementing to ensure you get the required amount.

Vitamin B-12 is also an important nutrient during your pregnancy, but it's difficult to find in most plant-based foods. Select fortified cereals or soy milk, brewer's yeast, and consider a multivitamin with an adequate level to ensure your body gets the amount it needs.

And though zinc is difficult to come by in a strict vegan or vegetarian diet, the need for it increases during pregnancy. Whole grains and legumes are wise choices to obtain this nutrient, but you again may need to supplement to make sure you're getting what you need.

As long as you eat a good variety of nutritious foods that provide the right amount of calories for a healthy weight gain, you should have no problem getting the vitamins and minerals your body needs at this marvelous time. And though many women do choose to take a prenatal vitamin daily, they should not be a substitute for good nutrition. Develop a cooperative relationship with your healthcare provider who supports your vegetarian lifestyle, and consider consulting a nutritionist when necessary.

Sample Daily Menu For Pregnant Vegetarians

Though your nutritional needs increase now that you're pregnant, your pregnancy vegetarian diet shouldn't have to change all that much. With some careful planning to ensure your caloric, vitamin, and mineral needs are met, you can still enjoy a rich variety of nutrient-dense delicious foods and help give your baby a nutritious jump-start. Consider the following daily menu for ideas and inspiration.

Breakfast:
1/2 cup oatmeal with maple syrup
1 slice whole wheat toast with fruit spread
1 cup soy milk
1/2 cup calcium and vitamin D fortified orange juice

Snack:
1/2 whole wheat bagel with margarine
Banana

Lunch:
Veggie burger on whole wheat bun with mustard and catsup
1 cup steamed collard greens
Medium apple
1 cup soy milk

Snack:
3/4 cup ready-to-eat cereal with 1/2 cup blueberries 1 cup soy milk

Dinner:
3/4 cup tofu stir-fried with 1 cup vegetables
1 cup brown rice
Medium orange

Snack:

Whole grain crackers with 2 Tbsp peanut butter

4 ounces apple juice

If morning sickness is giving you fits during your pregnancy, try eating low fat, high carbohydrate nutrient-dense foods. These are digested more quickly and stay in the stomach for less time giving less time for queasiness. Remember to eat often. Sometimes nausea is really hunger in disguise.

Be sure to drink juice, water, or soy milk if you can't eat solid food. Keep trying to eat whatever you can. If you're unable to eat or drink the appropriate amounts of foods or fluids for 24 hours or more, get in touch with your healthcare provider.

Going Vegetarian During Your Pregnancy

Now that you're pregnant, you're wondering if your decision to become vegetarian can still be carried out successfully during your pregnancy. And while it is possible for you to obtain all the nutrients your body will need during pregnancy through a well-planned, nutrient-dense vegetarian diet, careful planning and observation will be crucial to your overall success transitioning to vegetarianism during your pregnancy. In other words: take it slow and be smart!

A good vegetarian diet has a wide variety of fresh fruits, vegetables, grains, beans, lentils, and nuts and some eggs and dairy or their equivalent if you so choose. Fast food, highly processed junk foods, and canned fruits and vegetables are eaten rarely if at all. It's imperative that you make wise food choices at this crucial time, since a pregnant woman only needs approximately 300 more calories per day and about 10-16 extra grams of protein; however, the body's need for certain nutrients increases significantly. Every bite you take is important when you're pregnant. While the RDAs (recommended daily allowances) for almost all nutrients increase, especially important are folic acid, iron, zinc, and vitamin B-12. Attention to adequate amounts of vitamin B-12 is crucial for vegetarians who choose not to eat eggs and dairy.

Work closely with your healthcare professional during this transition. The changeover from a meat-eating to a vegetarian diet can be rough on your body as it actually goes through a detoxification process during the transition. So, you want to ensure your baby is getting all the nutrients it needs at this time, and is growing and developing at a healthy rate. Start very slowly; perhaps only one or two days per week eating a vegetarian diet. Gradually work in soy- and plant-based proteins into your diet, and little by little use them to replace proteins obtained from eating meat products. Be sure to adequately supplement your diet with a quality prenatal supplement, and get adequate amounts of exercise and exposure to sunlight to promote your body to naturally produce vitamin D.

With careful planning, observation, and your healthcare professional's guidance, the transition to vegetarianism during your pregnancy can be a cleansing and healthy start for both you and your baby to a lifetime of optimal health.

The Healing Effects A Vegetarian Diet Has On Your Post-Baby Body

The breastfeeding vegetarian diet doesn't vary all that much from the pregnancy vegetarian diet. Protein recommendations are the same, vitamin B-12 recommendations are higher, and the recommendations for iron and calories are lower than during pregnancy. But the key in ensuring your healthy vegetarian diet is also helping you recover from the stresses of giving birth and taking care of your newborn is healthy fats. Healthy fats and oils play active roles in every stage of the body's healing, building, and maintenance processes. In fact, they are as important to an active individual's body as amino acids, minerals, and vitamins. Healthy fats and oils help convert light and sound into electrical nerve impulses, remove potentially toxic substances from sensitive tissue, and provide strength to cell membranes.

The key is in balancing fats from a variety of foods. All foods that contain dietary fat contain a combination of fatty acids-the chemical building blocks of fat. Learning about the mixture of fatty acids in your diet will help you figure out how to choose foods with the good fats and avoid those foods that contain the bad fats.

For healthy fats, look to monounsaturated and polyunsaturated fatty acids. These can readily be found in a variety of vegetables, oils, and nuts, such as avocados, almonds, and olive oil. These help your body to resist attack from free radicals, which are specially formed types of atoms that can damage your body's cells when they react with DNA or cell membranes-better than other fats and thus are less prone to stick to your arteries.

Polyunsaturated fats occur in food either as omega-3 or omega-6 fatty acids. The key to eating healthy polyunsaturated fats is to maintain the right balance of omega-3 acids-found abundantly in flax, walnuts and canola oil-with omega-6 acids, found in vegetable oils such as corn, safflower and sesame.

Sample Vegetarian Diet Including Essential Fatty Acids To Promote

Healing

Fats are an essential part of any well-balanced diet, including a vegetarian diet. Fats are made of smaller units - called fatty acids. These fatty acids may be saturated, monounsaturated or polyunsaturated. Saturated and monounsaturated fats are not necessary in a vegetarian diet as they can be made in the human body. However, two polyunsaturated fatty acids - linoleic acid (omega 6) and linolenic acid (omega 3) - cannot be manufactured by the body and must be provided in the diet.

Fortunately, they are widely available in vegetarian/vegan plant foods. Evidence is increasing that omega 6 (found in foods like vegetable oils such as corn, safflower and sesame) and especially omega 3 (found in flax, walnuts, avocados, almonds and olive and canola oil) fats are beneficial for a range of conditions, including heart disease, cancer, immune system deficiencies and arthritis.

Healthy fats and oils play active roles in every stage of the body's healing, building, and maintenance processes. In fact, they are as important to an active individual's body as amino acids, minerals, and vitamins. Healthy fats and oils help convert light and sound into electrical nerve impulses, remove potentially toxic substances from sensitive tissue, and provide strength to cell membranes.

The following vegetarian menu sample shows how easy it is for essential fatty acids to be a part of your every day vegetarian diet.

Breakfast:

1 bagel with 2 tsp vegan margarine, 1 medium orange, 1 cup Cheerios cereal, and 1 cup soymilk

Lunch:

Sandwich of hummus made with 3/4 cup chickpeas and 2 teaspoons tahini (a sandwich spread made from ground sesame seeds) on 2 slices of whole wheat bread with 3 slices of tomato and ½ sliced avocado

Dinner:

1 cup of cooked pasta with 1/4 cup marinara sauce, 1/3 cup carrot sticks, 1 cup cooked broccoli (frozen or fresh), and 1 whole wheat roll

Snack:

1/2 cup almonds, and 1 cup soymilk

What To Feed Your Vegetarian Baby

It goes without saying that the earliest food for any baby, including a vegan baby, is breast milk. It benefits your baby's immune system, offers protection against infection, and reduces the risk of allergies. Be especially careful that you are getting enough vitamin B-12 when breastfeeding. Also, ensure your infant receives at least 30 minutes of sunlight exposure per week to stimulate the body to produce adequate amounts of vitamin D, since human milk contains very low levels.

The iron content of breast milk is also generally low, no matter how good the mother's diet is. The iron which is in breast milk is readily absorbed by the infant, however. The iron in breast milk is adequate for the first 4 to 6 months or longer. After the age of six months, it is recommended iron supplements are introduced.

Soy milk, rice milk, and homemade formulas should not be used to replace breast milk or commercial infant formula during the first year. These foods do not contain the proper ratio of protein, fat, and carbohydrate, nor do they have enough of many vitamins and minerals to be used as a significant part of the diet in the first year.

Many people use iron-fortified infant rice cereal as the first food. Cereal can be mixed with expressed breast milk or soy formula so the consistency is fairly thin. Formula or breast milk feedings should continue as usual. Start with one cereal feeding daily and work up to 2 meals daily or 1/3 to 1/2 cup. Oats, barley, corn, and other grains can be ground in a blender and then cooked until very soft and smooth. These cereals can be introduced one at a time. However, they do not contain much iron, so iron supplements should be continued.

When baby becomes used to cereals, fruit, fruit juice, and vegetables can be introduced. Fruits and vegetables should be well mashed or puréed. Mashed banana or avocado, applesauce, and puréed canned peaches or pears are all good choices. Mild vegetables such as potatoes, carrots, peas, sweet potatoes, and green beans should be cooked well and mashed. Grain foods such as soft, cooked pasta or rice, soft breads, dry cereals, and crackers can be added when baby becomes better at chewing.

Traditional Meat

How did our family traditions become centered around eating meat? Think about it. When we think of Thanksgiving, we think of turkey. If we eat pork, then New Year's celebrations often revolve around pork and sauerkraut. At Christian Easter, the traditional meal is ham. And in the summer, we wait for that first hamburger or steak on the grill.

How did that happen to a species that was designed to eat vegetables and fruits, nuts, berries and legumes?

We can imagine that eating meat was initially an opportunistic event, born of the need to survive. The taste of cooked meat, plus the sustained energy that came from eating high-fat meat products made primitive sense even to earliest man.

Initially, finding cooked animal meat, from a forest fire, would have been cause for celebration. It's something everyone in a clan would have participated in eating together. When man learned to hunt and moved to a hunting orientation, rather than a hunter-gatherer orientation, he would have done this in groups. They would have had to hunt in teams, and killing an animal for food would have been a group effort. Hunting and killing an animal meant food not just for the individual, but for the clan, and would have been cause for celebration when the hunters brought the food home.

If they brought the animal back to the clan, it would have taken a group effort to skin the animal and tear or cut the meat from the carcass. Everyone would have participated in this, and subsequently, shared in the rewards of their work.

It's easy to see how, once we didn't have to hunt for meat, but could buy it, the need for gathering and celebration was deeply ingrained in our natures. We celebrate the seasons and life's events with family and friends, and because those early celebrations involved eating meat, that tradition has continued to modern times.

Variety Is The Spice Of Your Vegetarian Child's Diet

Eating habits are set in early childhood. Choosing a vegetarian diet can give your child—and your whole family—the opportunity to learn to enjoy a variety of wonderful, nutritious foods. Offer your child a wide variety of grains, fruits, vegetables, nuts, seeds, and soy products, keep it simple and make it fun, and they'll learn good eating habits that will last them a lifetime.

Children raised on fruits, vegetables, whole grains, and legumes grow up to be slimmer and healthier and even live longer than their meat-eating friends. It is much easier to build a nutritious diet from plant foods than from animal products, which contain saturated fat, cholesterol, and other substances that growing children can do without. As for essential nutrients, plant foods are the preferred source because they provide sufficient energy and protein packaged with other health-promoting nutrients such as fiber, antioxidant vitamins, minerals and healthy fats.

The complex carbohydrates found in whole grains, beans, and vegetables provide the ideal energy to fuel a child's busy life. Encouraging the consumption of brown rice, whole wheat breads and pastas, rolled oats, and corn, as well as the less common grains barley, quinoa, millet, and others, will boost the fiber and nutrient content of a child's diet. In addition, it will help steer children away from desiring sugary sweet drinks and treats.

And though children need protein to grown, they don't need high-protein, animal-based foods. Different varieties of grains, beans, vegetables, and fruits supplies plenty of protein, making protein deficiency very unlikely.

Very young children need a bit more healthy fats in their diets than their parents. Healthier fat sources include soybean products, avocados, and nut butters. Parents will want to make sure their child's diet includes a regular source of vitamin B-12, which is needed for healthy nerve function and blood. Vitamin B-12 is abundant in many commercial cereals, fortified soy and rice milks, and nutritional yeast. Growing children also need iron found in a variety of beans and green, leafy vegetables and when coupled with the vitamin C in fruits and vegetables, iron absorption is enhanced.

Putting Your Vegetarian Toddler On The Fast Track To Health

Though many people have the idea that feeding a toddler a vegetarian diet isn't safe, so long as parents take care to make sure that all the appropriate nutrients are met, it's actually quite healthy. Some benefits to a lifelong, proper vegetarian diet include a lower risk of heart disease, high blood pressure, diabetes and obesity.

The main problem with vegetarianism and toddler nutrition is making sure your child gets enough nutrients and calories. Calorie consumption is important for ensuring your toddler has the energy he needs to play hard and grow.

It can be challenging to develop a well-rounded vegetarian toddler menu that provides enough protein and iron. Since toddlers already have such a small appetite, it can be difficult to get them to eat enough vegetables or beans to receive all of their nutrients. Therefore, it is important that vegetarian children are served nutrient-dense foods.

Soybeans and tofu are a great source of protein for adults and children over four. For toddlers, though, it shouldn't be used as their main source of protein. In this instance, compliment the tofu or soybeans that you serve with soymilk that has been fortified with vitamins and minerals. Not only will this help provide some protein, it will also help your toddler's nutrition by providing calcium, and vitamins A and D, which can often be hard to get in a vegan diet.

Iron can be found in many vegetarian-friendly foods. Kidney beans, lima beans, green beans, and spinach are all excellent sources of iron. However, unlike iron derived from animal sources, iron from vegetables can be hard for your body to absorb properly. But serving a vitamin C rich food with those beans or spinach can make the iron easier for your toddler to absorb. Some great sources of vitamin C include tomatoes, oranges, broccoli, red peppers, and cantaloupe.

While it is possible to raise a healthy vegan, it can take a bit more work. You may need to supplement your toddler's diet to ensure they get all the nutrition that they need. Vitamin B-12 can be especially difficult for vegans to get enough of. While vegetables contain some B-12 vitamins, the body does not easily absorb these. Your toddler's healthcare provider can help you decide on a B-12 suitable for toddlers.

A diet that does not allow for calcium can also be detrimental to your child's health. Calcium helps to make bones stronger and aids in proper growth and development. Choose soymilk that is calcium-fortified, but be sure it's also fortified with other nutrients that your toddler needs for good nutrition.

Sample Menu Items For Your Growing Vegetarian Toddler

Vegetarian child. The term almost sounds like an oxymoron we've joked about through the years, like jumbo shrimp. The words just don't seem to go together! It's not as unnatural as it may sound. Actually, kids are almost natural vegetarians. It's imperative that you offer your growing vegetarian child a wide variety of fruits, vegetables, grains, nuts, seeds, and soy based proteins to ensure they have the energy and nutrients needed to grow up strong, healthy, and happy. Consider including items in your daily menu planning for a well-rounded, nutrient-dense healthy diet:

2.5-3 cups fortified soymilk
1/4-1/2 cup iron-fortified cereal
2-5 servings grains (1/2 slice bread, 1/4 cup cooked rice, pasta, quinoa, etc)

2-3 servings veggies (1/2 cup salad or raw veggies, 1/4 cup cooked veggies—bear in mind that the younger your child is, cooked vegetables might be easier for them to chew and digest, then introduce raw veggies as they grow older.)

2-3 servings fruit (1/2 fresh fruit, 1/4 cup cooked fruit, 1/4 cup juice)

2 servings protein foods (1/4 -1/3 cup cooked beans/lentils, a slice or so of calcium-fortified tofu, or peanut or almond butter – be sure that nut butters are fed to children who've been tested and shown not to have nut allergies; if you're unsure, wait until your child's healthcare provider has had the opportunity to test for such allergies in your child before trying them)

Vitamin B-12 source - nutritional yeast, breast milk, formula, fortified soy milks and cheeses

Vitamin D - sunlight, breast milk, formula, fortified soy milk
Omega-3 Essential Fatty Acids - flaxseed oil, freshly ground flaxseed

And here's some finger-food friendly options for your growing vegetarian toddler:

Fresh or frozen mango
Fresh or frozen peaches/nectarines/plums

Cubed avocado

Tofu (put in microwave or steam for 10-30 seconds

Fresh or frozen peas

Pasta that is slightly overcooked

Cubed soy or rice cheeses

Canned beans- black, garbanzo, black eyed peas, or kidney

Toast, cut into little pieces

Ideas For Adding Some Variety To Your Vegetarian Lifestyle

When you're planning a healthy vegetarian diet, you're only limited by your imagination. It's important to incorporate a wide variety of whole grains, legumes, vegetables and fruits in different meals, including seeds and nuts. Variety is the spice of life, and it will help ensure your vegetarian diet is nutrient-dense, interesting, and fun! Aim for variety, even when you serve favorite entrees over and over again, by serving different side dishes, snacks and desserts.

Be creative in planning meals. Boost your consumption of beans and vegetables by eating these foods at lunch time rather than just for dinner. Make it a goal to serve a vegetable every day for lunch and two for dinner. Plan a meal around a vegetable. A baked potato can be a hearty entree; serve it with baked beans, a sauce of stewed tomatoes or a few tablespoons of salsa. Or make a simple meal of sautéed vegetables and pasta.

Try new foods often. Experiment with a variety of grains such as quinoa, couscous, bulgur, barley, and wheat berries. Try fruits and vegetables that are popular in different international cuisines, such as bok choy. Accentuate the positive. Focus more on healthy foods that fit into a vegetarian plan instead of foods to avoid. If you're unsure how to include a new food into your vegetarian diet, ask the produce manager at your local grocer or health food store for ideas on how to prepare it. The internet can be a great resource for new recipe and preparation ideas. But be sure that you're building your menu on a strong plant food base. Make them the core of your diet.

Don't stress about getting enough protein. As long as calories are sufficient and the diet is varied, vegetarians easily meet protein needs. Grains, beans, vegetables, and nuts all provide protein. Vegetarians do not need to eat special combinations of foods to meet protein needs. However, it is important to be aware of fat. Even vegetarians can get too much fat if the diet contains large amounts of nuts, oils, processed foods, or sweets.

Tips For A Vibrant Vegetarian Holiday Filled With Variety

Planning a beautiful yet nutrient-dense, delicious holiday meal for both your meat eating and vegetarian guests can be a little daunting at first, but it can also bring out your creativity! Many side dishes you make can be easily made vegetarian, with little difference in taste.

The first step in planning accordingly would be to find out which of your guests are vegetarian, and what kind of vegetarian they are. Do they eat eggs or cheese? If so, you'll have a few more possibilities. If they don't, that's okay, you'll still have plenty of options to work with. If you're new to the vegetarian lifestyle and aren't quite sure where to start, ask for some input or help from your vegetarian guests. They may have some great recipe ideas, shortcuts, or simple tricks of the trade they can share with you to make your holiday meal preparation go smoothly.

For instance, you can substitute vegetable broth for chicken broth, or simply leave the meat or meat drippings out of vegetables and soups. This will also cut down on the fat content. It's also very simple to divide some of the dishes, making one portion meatless, using the same vegetarian ingredients just mentioned.

Most importantly, keep in mind that the holidays are about peace, love, and understanding. With this in mind, please try not to be judgmental of what people you love choose to eat if you are not vegetarian yourself. Support your family member or friend's choice to eat vegetarian. Seize the opportunity to learn from them. Incorporate ideas from a vegetarian lifestyle into your own to ensure your family is eating a variety nutrient-dense, delicious fruits, vegetables, grains, seeds, and nuts at every meal.

Veggies Take Center State At Your 4th Of July Cookout

Your annual 4th of July cookout is quickly approaching. Whether you're expecting vegetarian guests, you've newly transitioned to vegetarianism yourself, or you'd just like to incorporate more meatless recipes to give some variety to your cookout menu, there are all kind of ways to prepare meatless options.

Before beginning, remember that most vegetarian foods are more fragile than meat, and do not contain as much fat. Therefore, clean and well-lubricated grill is essential to successfully grilling vegetables. It'd be a shame for those beautifully grilled peppers to stick to the grill!

Traditionally, vegetables have been considered a side dish in most meals, but at a cookout they can take center stage as the entrée. Almost any kind of vegetable is great for grilling. Complement your meal by serving them over pasta, rice or polenta. You can also make them into extraordinary sandwiches with a soy-based cheese and some freshly baked rolls or bread. Cut the vegetables lengthwise into thin slices in the case of zucchini and eggplant, or into thick rings, in the case of onions, tomatoes and peppers. If you'd rather have your veggies in handy bite-size pieces for serving with pasta and the like, try using a special pan for the grill with small holes that keep the veggies from falling through the grill and being lost. And probably the easiest way to grill vegetables on the grill is shish-ka-bob style!

Don't forget to balance out those grilled vegetables with some fresh fruit salads, perfectly chilled and juicy. Watermelon, strawberries, grapes, and citrus fruits all complement one another well in a delightful fruit salad prepared with non-dairy whipped cream. Also use fruits to experiment with some fun smoothies and slushies for the kids – they're fun and better for them than sugary sodas.

Tips For A Tasty Vegetarian Thanksgiving

If you're hosting Thanksgiving at your house and are expecting vegetarian guests this year, don't worry about preparing one large meat eating meal, and another separate vegetarian meal. Most vegetarians do not require a 'meat equivalent' at Thanksgiving. Yes, traditionally Thanksgiving has largely about the food. But more importantly it's about family, togetherness, happiness and peace. And if this is your first Thanksgiving after transitioning to a vegetarian lifestyle, try some of these ideas to incorporate healthy food preparation into your meal that your vegetarian guests, and you as host, will be thankful for this Thanksgiving:

- Bake some stuffing outside of the turkey.

- Make a small portion of vegetarian gravy.

- Keep cooking utensils separate to prevent "cross-contamination" between meat foods and vegetarian foods.

- When recipes are adaptable, use substitutions like vegetarian broth, soy margarine (the formulations without whey are suitable for vegans), soy milk, and kosher marshmallows which are made without gelatin.

- Use vegetable oils instead of animal fats for frying, and vegetable shortening like Crisco for pie crust.

- Read ingredients lists carefully on pre-packaged foods, being aware of terms like gelatin, whey, and "natural flavors" that can be animal-derived.

- Prepare plenty of vegetable and fruit side dishes, but leave them plain.

- Offer plenty of breads, beverages, fresh fruits, and non-gelatin desserts, which are suitable without modification for most vegetarians.

- Invite your vegetarian guest to prepare a "Tofurky" or vegetarian 'turkey equivalent' entrée to share with you the rest of your guests, or if you're hosting Thanksgiving, prepare a small one. Your meat-eating guests might just be curious enough to want to try it!

- Ask your vegetarian guest for help, tips, or recipes that would complement their vegetarian choice. You may find that your guest offers to help out in the kitchen or bring a dish from home. Please don't take a dish from home as an insult to your cooking; take it as a desire to share traditions at Thanksgiving. Even meat-eating homes can benefit from a healthy, nutrient-dense vegetarian recipe idea any time of the year!

- Most importantly – make TONS of new, delicious (not overly cooked) vegetables that are perfectly in season like squashes, sweet potatoes, and green beans, etc.

Remembering The Reasons For A Vegetarian Season

Christmas is a season of peace, love and harmony. It's a time that brings families and friends together to reconnect and find comfort and happiness being together. It's also about respect for fellow man, appreciating and embracing one another's differences. Take some time over the holiday season to reflect on the reasons for your choice to become vegetarian, and enforce your commitment and dedication to the vegetarian lifestyle. What reason, or reasons, helped you decide that vegetarianism was the right choice for you?

Was it Economic? A meat-based diet can be very expensive. Fresh produce bought in season can be very affordable, and can be prepared (dried, canned, frozen) so that it can be enjoyed later in the season.

Was it Ethical? Did you choose not to eat meat because of the meat processing techniques are incredibly cruel to animals? Do some research on the internet or the library, visit the PETA website, and you're very likely to find more credible reasoning that affirms your choice.

Was it Environmental? A vegetarian lifestyle is more environmentally friendly – large ranching operations cause topsoil erosion, coyotes and other natural predators are destroyed routinely to protect herds of cows which are only slaughtered anyway later on, and commercial fishing operations are damaging the ocean's ecosystems.

Was it to Improve Your Health? Eating a vegetarian diet has been shown to be a very healthy lifestyle, as it helps fight heart disease, reduces cancer risks, lowers cholesterol, helps lower blood sugar and reverse the effects of diabetes, lowers the obesity risk, and reduces the risk of osteoporosis, as meat consumption has been shown to promote bone loss. And remember: just because it's Christmas, it doesn't mean you can't enjoy many of the same wonderful holiday treats you've become accustomed to, as long as they are prepared with your vegetarian lifestyle in mind. Breads, cookies prepared with vegetable shortening, egg substitutes, whole grain flours and soymilks, numerous choices for vegetable dishes and salads can all be enjoyed by both vegetarians and non-vegetarians alike during the holiday! So remember the reason for the season, reaffirm your reasoning for your life choice, and be proud of it, and of yourself.

<u>Variety In Your New Vegetarian Diet</u>

You've weighed your options carefully, studied the pros and the cons, and decided that the vegetarian lifestyle is right for you. But where do you start making the changes? Do you go 'cold turkey?' Do you adopt a more gradual approach to transitioning to vegetarianism? However you choose to make the change, you can begin to achieve the health benefits of vegetarianism by significantly cutting down on the amount of meats consumed, and making vegetables, fruits, legumes, and whole grains the focus of your meals.

Choose whole-grain products like whole wheat bread and flour, instead of refined or white grains. Eatawidevarietyoffoods,anddon'tbeafraidtotryvegetables,fruits,grains,breads, nuts, or seeds that you've never tried before. Experiment and explore! You may discover a new favorite or two, and learn fresh new ways to liven up more traditional vegetarian dishes. Many vegetarian foods can be found in any grocery store. Specialty food stores may carry some of the more uncommon items, as well as many vegetarian convenience foods. When shopping for food, plan ahead, shop with a list and read food labels. And if you decide to eat dairy products, choose non-fat or low-fat varieties, and limit your egg intake to 3-4 yolks per week.

Becoming a vegetarian can be as easy as you choose to make it. Whether you enjoy preparing delectable, delicious meals or choose quick and easy ones, vegetarian meals can be very satisfying. If you get in the habit of keeping the following on hand, meal preparation time will become a snap:

-Ready-to-eat, whole-grain breakfast cereals, and quick-cooking whole-grain cereals such as oatmeal, whole-grain breads and crackers, such as rye, whole wheat, and mixed grain and other grains such as barley and bulgur wheat

-Canned beans, such as pinto, black beans, and garbanzo beans

-Rice (including brown, wild, etc.) and pasta (now available in whole wheat, spinach, and other flavors) with tomato sauce and canned beans and/or chopped veggies

-Vegetarian soups like lentil, navy bean, or minestrone

-A wide variety of plain frozen vegetables, and canned and frozen fruit

-Fortified soymilks and soy cheeses, should you choose to not eat dairy

-A wide variety of fresh fruits and vegetables, which should be the core of any diet

As you learn to experiment with foods and learn that a meatless diet doesn't have to lack variety, you'll find your decision for vegetarianism was not only wise, but easy and fun come mealtime.

The Environmental Costs Of Factory Farming And Ranching

Long ago, eating meat was a good source of nutrition, since the use of hormones, pesticides and mass production methods was as yet unheard of. A family raised and processed their own livestock. Every morning the large golden eggs were plucked from the chicken's nests, which were lovingly cared for and fed healthy pesticide-free grains..

Today's factory farms use everything, but in the process they leave behind an environmental toll that generations to come will be forced to pay. Raising animals for food requires more that half the water used in the United States each year and one-third of all raw materials, including fossil fuels. This industry is the greatest polluter of our waters and is directly responsible for 85 percent of soil erosion. Our country's meat addiction is steadily poisoning and depleting our land, water and air.

Of all agricultural land in the United States, 87 percent is used to raise animals for food. That's 45 percent of the total land mass of the United States.

Methane is one of four greenhouse gases that contribute to global warming. The world's 1.3 billion cows produce one-fifth of all methane emitted into the atmosphere.

Raising animals for food causes more water pollution in the United States than any other industry because animals raised for food produce 20 times the excrement of the entire human population-230,000 pounds every second.

Of all raw materials and fossil fuels used in the United States, more than one-third is used to raise animals for food.

Rain forests are being destroyed at a rate of 125,000 square miles per year. The primary cause of deforestation is raising animals for food.

Coupled with the inhumane treatments of animals that are raised for human consumption, the costs of raising and processing these animals for human consumption is becoming too high. Make a commitment to reduce or eliminate meats from your diet, and learn to live from the plant foods the environment naturally provides. The animals and your conscience will be better for it.

Why Switch To Vegetarianism

If you've eaten meat and animal products your whole life, you might think, why switch to a vegetarian diet? You've lived your whole life eating eggs, hamburgers, hot dogs, and poultry, so why switch now?

There could be many reasons to switch. Start by looking in the mirror. Are you at a healthy weight? Do you look and feel good most of the time? Do you wake up energized? Or do you wake up tired and sluggish?

How is your general health? Is your blood pressure within a healthy range? Are your cholesterol and blood sugar ranges normal? If they're not, consider what you're eating on a daily basis.

How do you feel after eating? Do you feel energized, as if you've fed your body what it needs? Or are you tired and dragged out? Do you often need a nap after eating? Is that what food is supposed to do for us, make us tired and sleepy?

Not really. Food should nourish and feed the body and leave us energized and refreshed. The human body is a machine and needs fuel that keeps it running in peak condition. When we're fat, with high blood pressure, Type II diabetes, high cholesterol and other unhealthy conditions, it's like a car engine that hasn't been tuned or isn't running on the optimal type of gasoline it needs to run efficiently. Your body is the same way. It needs the right kind of fuel to run at peak efficiency, and when you're eating high-fat meat, or meat that's been fed antibiotics throughout its life, that's simply not the kind of fuel the human body evolved to run on.

Try eating vegetarian for a week or a month. See if you don't feel different, more mentally acute and more physically fit and energized. At least reverse the portion sizes you've been eating, and make meat more of a side dish, if you can't stop eating meat altogether. Even that change can make a big difference in your overall health and well-being.

Nourishing Our Body, Nourishing Our Spirit

Many times our choice to become vegetarian isn't only for health, environmental, or economical reasons, but also spiritual. There is a heartfelt connection between vegetarianism and the deeper side of nourishment. We must learn to nourish ourselves not only physically, but also spiritually.

The subject of nutrition is not simply a question of the food we eat at meals. Besides nutrients, foods contain scents, colors and invisible particles that attract pure light, light that is so essential for our joyful life and well-being. The choice we make is therefore always of consequential sig nif icance.

Grains, fruits and vegetables naturally grow and flourish in sunlight, and you could deduce they are actually their own form of light. In order to develop the qualities of the heart, we must eat not only peacefully, but consciously. Therefore it makes sense to consume food that is nourished by sunlight. As a result, our emotions and our essence are illuminated and nourished as well.

It's long been said that your body is your temple and everything that enters that temple has a direct result in who we become. Therefore, when we choose to nourish our bodies with healthful, nutrient-dense plant foods from the earth, we are in turn nourishing our souls, our spirit, and our being. The quality of your food and its physical properties not only transforms our emotions and mind, but can actually change your appearance and personality.

By focusing our diet on fresh fruits and vegetables that are in season and organically produced, we are in turn connecting with nature and learning to live in harmony with it. By committing and devoting ourselves to a vegetarian lifestyle, we've also committed to nourishing our souls and our inner well-being. You can't ask for a more perfect health food than that!

PETA

People have different motivations for eating a vegetarian diet. For many people, it's a health issue. They need to reduce their weight, bring down their blood pressure and cholesterol, and manage their blood sugars. A vegetarian diet helps them do this.

For others, it's also moral and ethical decision not to eat animal products. Through the centuries, we've become accustomed to thinking of man as superior to all other animals on the planet. We use animals for food, clothing, shoes, belts or other accessories. We use them for scientific experiments. We discount their place on the earth and consider that animals are here to serve us and our needs.

PETA stands for People for the Ethical Treatment of Animals, and is an organization devoted to changing that mindset among humans. They are against using animals for food or for clothing, especially for what they consider the needless or particularly inhumane use of animals, such as killing or trapping them for their fur.

They are passionate about their cause. In their own words, PETA believes that animals have rights and deserve to have their best interests taken into consideration, regardless of whether they are useful to humans. Like you, they are capable of suffering and have an interest in leading their own lives; therefore, they are not ours to use—for food, clothing, entertainment, experimentation, or any other reason.

We are supposedly an evolved society. But how evolved can a society be that thrives on the suffering of animals? In his excellent book, When Elephants Weep, author Jeffrey Masson explores the emotional lives of animals and presents compelling evidence for it. As a species, we must begin to re-evaluate our place on this earth and where we fit in relation to every other creature that inhabits it. PETA believes this as well and is a passionate advocate for the rights of animals.

Caged Chickens And Hormones

If most of us thought about the conditions in which chickens used for meat and eggs are raised and slaughtered, we'd become vegetarian on the spot. Egg-laying chickens can be raised in cages with 6 chickens to a cage, each chicken getting only 67 square inches of space for its lif etime.

Unless they're certified and labeled as being free-range or organic or natural, they might have been fed growth hormones to get them to slaughter faster, and antibiotics to combat the diseases which come from being raised in cramped and less-than-clean conditions.

And consider what the recommendations are for cleaning up after touching poultry? It's recommended to clean surfaces with bleach to remove bacteria, and to wash your hands thoroughly after touching a chicken.

Do you really want to put something into your body that requires bleach to clean up after? Something that needs to be cooked to specific temperatures to be sure you've destroyed any bacteria that could make you sick?

Chickens and turkeys have become so mass-produced and injected with antibiotics and hormones that there's no taste to it anymore, so why bother? Even the most humanely treated chicken has either been stunned in a salt-water brine before being beheaded. In John Robbins excellent book and video, Diet for a Small Planet, he shows us pictures of chickens being grabbed in groups by the neck and thrown into cages. Can you really consider eating a chicken with that vision in your head?

Any means of mass-producing animals for human consumption is by its very nature unhealthy and cruel for the animals, and unhealthy for humans as well. Even if you're of the opinion that man is a natural hunter, how natural is it to eat an animal that's been raised in captivity and fed a diet of hormones and antibiotics?

Cow Slaughterhouses

Even if you don't eat meat, you might think drinking or using milk is part of a vegetarian diet. We all have images of farmers pumping milk by hand, and it seems a natural part of life and a benign use of the cow. But we don't really think much about it at all, do we?

Do you know how a cow raised for producing milk lives its life? Like most animals used for mass consumption, a milk cow lives in cramped and often filthy conditions. It is fed hormones to stimulate its reproductive processes, because that's what a mother's milk is for – to feed its baby. As soon as a calf is born though, it's taken from its mother. A male calf often goes to a terrible fate to be raised for veal; a female calf often has the same fate as its mother.

Often the cows mourn for their babies. They'll be seen bellowing for them and looking for them. Mass producing milk for human consumption has disrupted the natural order of things.

The cows are fed hormones to continue to stimulate milk production. The electric pumps are painful to the cow's udders. With the hormone stimulation, cows are forced to produce 10 times more milk than they would ordinarily.

When their milk-producing days are over, the cows are then slaughtered for ground beef. It also takes enormous natural resources to feed and water all these cows. The water table is being depleted to sustain this enormous industry. And the waste produced by all these large animals is having a detrimental effect on the environment.

We really don't need to consume milk after a certain age. Why would we continue to support this industry that's built on animal suffering? To really top it off, humans are not meant to drink cow milk. Calves are meant to drink cow milk and we humans are meant to drink human milk. Our bodies were not designed to digest the proteins in cow milk – so why bother? Especially when you can get more calcium from a green, leafy vegetable?

Veal

There are few issues that make a more compelling argument for a vegetarian diet than that of veal and how it's produced. While the meat industry is, by its very nature cruel and inhumane, the veal industry is the worst.

Baby calves are taken from their mothers, often at just one day old. They're kept in pens that prevent movement, to keep their muscles soft. To produce the pale, soft veal that is so highly prized by gourmets, the calves are fed a liquid that's deficient in iron and fiber that creates an anemia in the animal.

The confinement in which they live for their short lives creates a significant level of chronic stress for the animal and they're subsequently given much higher levels of medications that can be harmful to humans. The confinement makes them weak, often unable to stand. We treat criminals who have committed the most vicious crimes imaginable more humanely than we treat innocent calves.

Why would anyone want to consume meat that's delivered to the table infused with the suffering of animals? What culinary experience can ever be worth it when you know what the animal, especially a calf, has to go through?

At age 20 weeks, the calf is then slaughtered. All the meat we eat has been mass produced and slaughtered. Their life is inhumane and their death is inhumane, in addition to which it's becoming less and less healthy for us to eat. Veal is the premier example of this industry. Changing to a vegetarian diet not only is a much more healthy way to eat, it's way of living in balance with the earth. It may have been one thing centuries ago to hunt for meat because it was a means for survival. Today's mass-produced meat industry is nothing like that and is more a cause of illness and poor health than it is for survival or nutrition.

The Difference Between Vegan & Vegetarian

Whether you are preparing meals for someone else or thinking about changing your own diet you need to know the difference between a vegetarian and a vegan. Put simply, a vegetarian is someone who does not eat meat or fish and a vegan is someone who eats no animal products at all.

There are, of course, people who eat meat and fish occasionally. They may be in the process of changing to a full vegetarian diet or concerned to reduce their intake of saturated fat. They might be considered as semi-vegetarians.

Some vegetarians will consume milk and dairy products but will not eat eggs. They are often called lacto-vegetarians. They would be vegans except that they include milk in their diet.

Other vegetarians avoid milk, but will eat eggs. They are ovo-vegetarians. They would be vegans if they did not consume eggs.

At some points many vegetarians may pass through one or other of these stages if they are moving towards a fully vegan diet. A vegan avoids all animal products even in clothing. Some vegans will not even eat honey or yeast.

All these dietary preferences should be respected as valid life-style choices. The dietary preferences of your diners should be seen as a challenge rather than a chore.

It is possible to ensure a nutritious diet for an adult by following any of these plans. For a full vegan protein should come from pulses and grains combined in interesting combinations. Vegetarians will eat these dishes too. If you provide a variety of dishes your diners can make their own choices.

If you want to make the change to a fully vegan diet yourself it is best to begin with a gradual change. First work towards a vegetarian diet and then slowly move towards a vegan diet. Try not to be too hung up on the categories of vegan or vegetarian. Feel you way and enjoy getting the know the potential of the full vegetarian through to vegan spectrum.

What Is Vegetarian Cheese?

Cheese is often thought to be the ideal vegetarian food. It is frequently served as the only vegetarian choice on less imaginative menus.

But there are draw backs to regular cheese. Firstly, it is usually made with rennet. Rennet is an enzyme found in the stomachs of calves. So regular cheese is not a completely vegetarian product.

Some of the better retailers sell rennet-free cheese. It can be hard to find. You have to read the label carefully to check that cheese is rennet-free if you want a thoroughly vegetarian cheese.

The second problem is with the milk itself. Many vegetarians object to milk because cows are kept in intensive conditions and forced to calve every year so that they continue to produce milk. The unwanted male calves are shot at birth or kept for raising to produce veal. Even non-vegetarians have ethical objections to the nature of the dairy industry.

Many people, especially children, have health problems with milk. They may be lactose intolerant or concerned about their cholesterol levels. The modern diet tends to be high in dairy products and hence in animal fats that raise cholesterol.

But cheese is a favorite comfort food. It would be hard to give it up altogether. Are there vegetarian cheese alternatives to milk-based cheese?

Yes, there are. There are cheese-like soya products and there is cheese which is made from yeast.

Both these kinds of vegetarian cheese are lactose-free, free of saturated fat and will not raise cholesterol levels. Vegetarian cheese of either kind is the ideal product for those who are lactose intolerant or have been advised to follow a diet that is low in saturated fat because their cholesterol level is too high. Vegetarian cheese that is specially formulated to suit children's tastes can be purchased. Whether you choose soya cheese or cheese it is possible to make most of your favorite recipes with vegetarian cheese.

Is A Vegetarian Diet Safe For My Child?

If you are already a vegetarian or are planning to become a vegetarian and have children you may be concerned about whether a child can get enough nutrients on a vegetarian diet. It is commonly thought that a growing child needs meat and that children should not be vegetarian.

This is a fallacy. A child can eat a balanced vegetarian diet that provides all the nutrients needed for healthy growth. All that is required is some knowledge and planning on your part.

The main problem that emerges with a vegetarian diet where children are concerned is the same as with any other diet. Children's appetites are small in comparison to those of adults but their nutritional needs are high.

Children need small, frequent meals. Those meals need to be packed with nutrients. Otherwise they are just eating empty calories that can lead to obesity and other health problems.

Children are hungry when they come in from school for very good reasons. They are highly active and need to eat something right then and there. You should aim to keep a range of vegetarian snack ready.

Peanut butter on a slice of whole meal bread is ideal. It contains protein in the bread and the peanuts, which are both also a good source of zinc and calcium. If you select a brand of peanut butter that does not have sugar added to it this is healthy vegetarian snack.

Children are often reluctant to eat vegetables. They often seem too much like hard work to a small child. But few children will refuse a raw carrot cut up into sticks or grated carrot.

Pulses and grains are often unpalatable to children. But they can be mashed and formed into burgers that children love. Tomato sauce is always a favorite but avoid commercial sauces that have sugar added.

When you need to make children's food sweet use honey, unrefined sugar or pureed fruit. If a child does not become accustomed to sweet food it will not crave for the high levels of sugar that are found in many processed foods.

Iron is an important nutrient. In a vegetarian diet it is often derived from whole grains and leafy green vegetables. Where children are concerned it is often a good idea to include eggs in a vegetarian diet. They are a good source of iron.

Dairy produce such as milk, butter and cheese are valuable to the vegetarian child. Milk and cheese contain calcium, while butter contains essential fatty acids.

If your child cannot tolerate cow's milk then try goat's or sheep's milk which are often more digestible. The vegetarian child needs these sources of animal protein far more than an adult vegetarian.

It is not wise for a child to eat an entirely vegan diet. A child's body is still growing and it needs these animal products. If you source your eggs and dairy produce from farms that have high animal welfare standards then you need have no moral qualms.

A Vegetarian Holiday Season

If you have just gone vegetarian and are coming up to you first vegetarian holiday season, or if you find yourself cooking for a vegetarian this holiday season this is the article for you. A vegetarian holiday season need not be a gloomy series of substitutes for meat. Vegetarian fare can be festive in its own right.

A good nut roast is one of the delights of the vegetarian table. It takes some time to make so it is not something that vegetarians eat every day. But it takes much less time than a turkey.

You will need a selection of nuts and this is season of nuts. You will also need a food processor to grind them to a paste. The kind of nuts you use influences the flavor and color of the finished roast. Almonds, walnuts, cashews and some hazel nuts make an excellent vegetarian roast but be guided by your own tastes.

Grind the nuts and season them with salt, pepper and spices. Nutmeg is an ideal spice to use. Add some liquid such as vegetable stock and put the mixture into a tin. It should be baked in the oven for about an hour depending on size.

To accompany your vegetarian roast you will need sauces. Cranberry sauce is fine for vegetarians and non-vegetarians alike. An onion gravy made with vegetable stock will be eaten by all your guests.

Stuffing can be cooked in a separate dish. A combination of brown rice, dried fruit, chopped apples and spices will make a delicious accompaniment to the vegetarian roast. Just avoid adding meat fat. Rely on vegetable fat such as vegetarian suet.

For the visual aspect of a festive vegetarian meal you need to think about vegetables. Decorate your table with a variety of vegetable dishes. Baked squashes make a spectacular centre piece. Stuffed vegetables will show that you have taken that little bit of extra care about the meal.

If your meal is to be entirely vegetarian give the vegetables centre stage on your table. Their colors will delight the eyes of your diners. If you are entertaining vegetarians and non-vegetarians then the turkey will have to take pride of place. But all your guests will be able to tuck into the vegetarian dishes. Your meal may open their eyes to the world of vegetarian cuisine.

Remember that your vegetarian guests may be vegan. If you cannot ascertain this in advance then it will be as well to avoid the use of eggs and milk in your vegetarian dishes. A nut roast is often bound together with eggs but this is not essential. Cream sauces for dessert can be made from ground nuts. Cashews are always popular for this. Soya cream is also available.

When creating a cheese board take care to ensure that at least one cheese is made without rennet. Rennet comes from the lining of a cow's stomach and many vegetarians will not eat it. You might also like to have a few soy based cheeses. The soft soy based cheeses are an excellent option for guests who are watching their cholesterol levels as well as vegetarians and vegans.

The whole point of a holiday season is to share with friends and family. So if you are a non-vegetarian cooking for vegetarians or you are a vegetarian cooking for non-vegetarians make your festive table welcoming to all.

Some Statistics To Make You Think About Becoming A Vegetarian

The modern diet that relies heavily on meat and animal products is both unhealthy and wasteful of the earth's resources. By becoming a vegetarian you can contribute to the preservation of scarce resources and enjoy a healthier diet.

Meat and dairy production is a large scale industry that consumes vast amounts of grain and soy beans. Great tracts of forest have been cut down to provide grazing land for cattle contributing to the problem of global warming.

This resource hungry industry provides more food for the rich world than ever before. Yet many people go hungry while we in the rich industrialized world suffer from a whole range of diseases that are caused by eating too much meat and animal fat.

An estimated 800 million people live in the shadow of hunger. World hunger is increasing at a rate of 4 million a year.

If all the farm produce that is used to feed animals was used to feed people a vegetarian diet then no one in the world would need to be hungry. It takes 7.5 pounds of animal feed to produce 1 pound an pork and 5 pounds to produce 1 pound of chicken.

The American pork industry consumed 1.08 billion bushels of corn in 2004 and 265 million bushels of soybeans. This creates competition between humans and animals.

When we factor in the use of fossil fuels in the livestock industry for heating, lighting and transportation then the modern meat based diet begins to look totally unsustainable.

It takes one sixth of an acre of land to produce enough food for a vegan but more than three acres to feed a meat eater.

The high price of meat has encouraged many farmers in poor countries to shift away from their traditional crops that provided a largely vegetarian diet. They are increasingly producing livestock that they can sell to richer countries. Two-thirds of the grain that is exported from America goes to feed livestock.

Fishing does not use up grain. But it does not really provide a sustainable alternative to meat. Most of the world's major fisheries are in decline because of over fishing.

Fish farming is as costly in terms of feed as other forms of livestock farming. It takes 5 pounds of feed to produce a pound of fish.

The only real alternative to this waste of resources is for vegetarianism to become the diet of more people. A vegetarian is taking a stand against the wasteful use of resources.

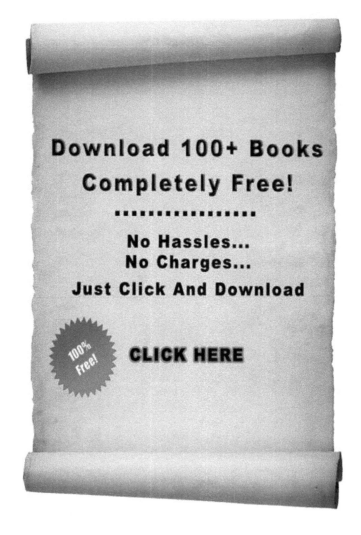

This Product Is Brought To You By